THE MAKING OF BILLY THE LIQUOR GUY

BILLY THE LIQUOR GUY

The Making of Billy the Liquor Guy

Published by:
Genius Book Publishing
PO Box 250380
Milwaukee Wisconsin 53225
GeniusBookPublishing.com

Hardcover ISBN: 978-1-958727-55-3

Paperback ISBN: 978-1-958727-54-6

241210 A5

CONTENTS

ACKNOWLEDGMENTS

Thank you to all promoters & book sellers that kept the sales of *Under Too Long* increasing, which allowed me the time to write *The Making of Billy the Liquor Guy*.

- Genius Publishing, for saying, when I asked about doing a second book, "You write it, we will publish it."
- Disruption Network. Zee, it all started with you.
- City of Utica, Mayor Rob, and Director of Productions, Paul Buckley
- Francis DiClemente, videographer, Sr. Professor, Syracuse University of Media Productions
- Barnes & Noble, New Hartford, N.Y
- Keaton and Lloyd Bookshop, Rome, NY
- Genesee Joe 92.7 FM, The Drive
- Talk of The Town 100.7 Rocco, Mark & Jay
- Keeler in the Morning, Bill Keeler, Jeff Monaski
- Marr-Logg House, John Maraffa
- Dan Falatico Jr., The Sausage King, and all his followers
- Nick Schmidt, young *Billy the Liquor Guy* local documentary

- Carol Jean, Wednesday Morning Club & MVILR & Tiny's.
- Jim Simpson, NYS Trooper, retired. Director of Promotion and Sales.
- Bill Cardette, Mayor of Dunkin.
- Peter Barone, videographer, for putting my website together and all your tech expertise in promoting both books.

- B, keep fighting brother.

DEDICATION

To all fallen first responders on 9/11 and the brothers and sisters we continue to lose, especially my good friend and coworker Chad Stevens

B. Asker who is fighting the fight of another 9/11 casualty

Chad & B. are beside me, Billy the Liquor Guy, on the cover of my first book. They always had my back.

Jeff Who & El Bobbo, featured on this cover, who kept me safe and sane while undercover.

Director Tom Stanton & Asst. Director Paul Rossi for the trust, confidence, and support when I strayed a bit.

Sr. Inv. Randy Cherubino who dealt with me on a daily basis where I might have pushed the envelope a few times.

It was my honor to work with all of you.

INTRODUCTION

I never thought I'd be a cop. I always wanted to be an investigator. I figured with a grandfather in the mafia teaching me about the criminal world, and utilizing this education on the streets of Utica, New York, called Sin City in the 1950s and '60s, I could keep out of harm's way. Which it did, especially while my grandfather was in prison. My grandfather taught me to never trust anybody, to read every room you walk into, and to always watch your back.

But to be an investigator, I would have to be a uniformed patrol officer for years. I was never one for structure, uniforms, or listening to directives from superiors.

Also, I did not want to deal with the politics in Utica at that time. Also, many of my frenemies were criminals, and I just did not want to deal with that bullshit.

I worked as an investigator for Utica, NY from 1975-1986. Then I took a break and bought a bar. I ran that bar for four years until I sold it.

After I got out of the bar business, I took a civil investigator's job out of town in New York City. A civil investigator has no police powers and does not carry a weapon. This lasted from 1990-'95. It improved the street skills I had already learned, let's just say, that were on the other side of the law. From this experience, I became interested in criminal investigation. Since I had a college degree along with this experience in civil investigation, I qualified for some non-uniform New York State jobs. I scored well on the Civil Service Exam, and was offered a job with New York State's Petroleum, Alcohol & Tobacco Bureau (PATB).

After attending training at the academy, I started in Syracuse, NY. On my first day I met the director, Bob Shepard. He came over to me, threw my badge, ID, and weapon on my desk, and said, "Now let's see if you can make it as a criminal investigator, not that civil bullshit stuff."

I liked him from the start.

He was up front and I could tell he was big on catching the bad guys.

Working for Mr. Shepard, "Shep," was my best work experience so far.

Until he left the agency.

Let's just say my life became much more interesting after that, and I found myself dealing with so much more bullshit.

[PART 1]
WORK LIFE

[1]
SHEP

Over the next three years after I joined, the Petroleum, Alcohol, and Tobacco Bureau, or PATB as it's known for short, began to rise from an agency that people didn't recognize to one that was gaining respect and attention. People now understood who we were and what we did, and a lot of that derived from the success we were having under Shep's watch.

Our agency was closing cases left and right, and thanks to our confidential informant, or CI, we were one step ahead of the game every damn time!

But, like everything else in life, success often comes with a green monster.

Fellow agencies began reaching out to Shep, seeking help protecting their operations. Shep was leery.

"You ever hear that term 'loose lips sink ships'?" he'd ask us. "That stands in play here. We're successful because we have our shit together. We're a tight unit, we respect each other, and we fight those goddamn bastards as a team. And that's as much as anyone needs to know. Understand?"

Our team was cool with Shep wanting to keep our strategies to ourselves. After all, we'd fought hard to be where we were.

At this point, I was now running the Plattsburgh office, with George and Brihiem still by my side. Our team had the freedom to run our shifts during times we saw fit. There was no nine-to-five or clock-in-and-take-a-break shit. We were in the field, on the move, and experiencing the freedom and adrenaline of being in the mix every single day.

During the height of our success, the higher-ups in the state office—or what I like to refer to as the Ivory Tower—began raining down on Shep. Somewhere, someone had a political agenda that they shoved up someone's ass. We were closing more cases than any agency in New York State, yet someone had made a complaint that we were doing so well because of our lack of sharing. Shep's knowledge and expertise, which he failed to provide other units and agencies, was now in question. Basically, they felt Shep held the secret formula, and when he didn't willingly hand that over to them, they grew spiteful and jealous.

"Why the fuck would I hide anything?" Shep asked the Powers That Be. "I'm out there doing the same shit as everyone else. I just happen to have an exemplary team. Our office is open to anyone who wants to come and spend a day with us. Hell, I'll be happy to show them how to motivate a team if that's what they need."

His answer wasn't enough. Within weeks, Shep had a

target on his back that wasn't aiming to go away. Shep was accused of failing to supervise the team and investigated for approving unnecessary expenses. As a former prosecutor and plain old smart man, Shep knew what they wanted. They were snooping around, looking for any reason to quietly push him out so they could appoint someone new in his spot. Someone they could puppet and control. Shep fought a good fight, refusing to give up our CI and our tactics until, after six months of ongoing investigations and stress, he finally handed in his badge and walked away.

"They're following my family now," he'd said during our final meeting. "I hope you all understand how disruptive that is to myself and my family. I'm never going to give them what they want, but I'm not going to give them the satisfaction of pushing me into a corner, either. Therefore, as of this afternoon, I'm leaving all of you to fight the good fight together. Don't let them break you. If anything, push it all on me. I can take it. After all, I don't have to come here day after day anymore. Once I leave this building, they no longer have any reason to bother me or my family. I'll be in the clear. You guys, however, may not be. Use me and keep kicking ass out there. Don't let my demise take away any of our success."

Shep handed in his badge and left our agency an hour later. There wasn't one member of our team who didn't feel resentful after that. They'd taken a good man who believed in what he did and who had fought to protect our country and sent him right back over to his former side.

Six months later, our team learned that Shep had resumed his career as an attorney. Only he wasn't just an ordinary attorney. He had become a Native Americans' defense attorney—

the one group of criminals our agency had been working to take down for years. Technically, you can't do that, suddenly fight for their side. It's seen as a form of espionage, if you will, and the state was all over it. Brimming with anger, the higher-ups smeared Shep's name across the state. They labeled him as a traitor and someone who was leaking information to the other side.

While they smeared his character, we kept quiet just like he asked. We continued to pursue our cases, played ignorant when people asked us questions, and based our lack of knowledge on Shep's need for privacy. It worked for a while, but eventually, everything takes its toll.

Shep's close companion and fellow investigator James was one of the first members of our team to take a secured job off the unit. He was also the one I needed to speak to about Shep's latest maneuver.

Sunday morning, I headed to my bedroom and dialed James.

"I've heard the rumors, too, Billy," he said. "It doesn't sound good on this end."

"I know," I admitted. "But I'm not ready to accept it. Shep wasn't that guy. He can't be working for the other side. He spent too much time with us. I feel like we're being set up."

"By who? Your informant? Your superiors? How many people have to tell you what's happening under your nose before you start to acknowledge it? You have to admit you're a little curious about what Shep's doing with them."

"James, he built this whole operation. He's responsible for thousands of dollars in arrests for the state, yet he just turns and leaves for the other side? I can't swallow that. I need something substantial, some proof, that what he's doing is designed to help them and hurt us."

"That I don't have for you, but I know the higher-ups do," he said. "There are pictures of Shep leaving the reservation on several occasions. From what I can tell, the rumors and accusations are true, and your team is about to suffer because of it."

"Suffer how? You were his friend, James."

"Correction. I thought I was his friend. He's lied to me as much as he has to you. Believe what you want, but he's working with the Native Americans. That makes your agency and all of our operations look like a joke. People are now wondering if what we did was a sham. They think we took money that was somehow tied in with the Native Americans all along, Billy."

"Yeah, the Native Americans allowed us to arrest them and confiscate their products and their cash for an inside deal. That sounds about as smart as the higher-ups' scenarios." Fury spewed inside me.

"Well, I don't know what the truth is, Billy. But I do know if Shep calls you, I would steer clear. At least for now. Hopefully, that will help strengthen your team."

"Well, I want to thank you for your time," I spat into the line. "Best five fucking minutes of wasted shit I've ever done. I really hope for your sake that Shep is who you say he is. If not, you've just proved yourself to be the yellow bastard I think you are."

My hands were shaking as I hung up the phone. If Shep had no allies left, then there was no one to call or reach out to for help.

I sat on the edge of my bed, my head in my hands,

thinking about everything I'd been through with Shep. I thought of the operations, the car races—Shep was a crazy bastard, and he used to create drag races for us between investigations. He saw it as a way to come together and blow off steam. He'd set a timer, give us a green flag, and yell like he was a NASCAR broadcaster for us to race back to our offices in New York from wherever we were investigating. More than once, he had us race from the Akwesasne reservation in Lake Placid, NY back to our Plattsburgh office, a distance of about 90 miles. Shep would watch out ahead for oncoming cars and warn us when it wasn't safe to pass on the two-lane roads of Route 191, aka the Highway of Death.

Shep always struck a deal with whoever made it back in the best time. Oftentimes that was money, coffee for a month, or sitting back on the next operation. But the prize didn't matter. Getting the respect from Shep and your fellow officers, and somehow making it back alive, was the ultimate prize.

As I sat there reminiscing about all the good times with Shep, I thought of all the office parties, the politicians, the arrests, the numerous awards we were presented, and all the talks he and I had had. Despite James' warning, if Shep was guilty and this was all a sham, I needed to be the one to venture out there and dig it up. I needed to see him face to face. However, before any of that could happen, there would be one more obstacle I would have to address.

To my surprise and horror, I returned to work on Monday to find two officers from Internal Affairs waiting for me. The duo was dressed in fine dark suits, shiny black shoes, and mismatched ties.

"Good morning, gentlemen," I said as I tried to walk by,

pretending to be oblivious as to who they were and why they were there. Any schmuck worth his salt can spot an asshole from Internal Affairs, and any sucker immediately knows just who or what directed their attention to you. I knew my "who" was James and my "what" was Shep. So much for trusting anyone.

"William," they said, rising from their seats as I passed. "We're here to speak with you."

"Oh," I said, continuing my clueless, aloof act. "I apologize. You guys are?"

"Officer Ryan," the heavyset suit said, shaking my hand. His palms left a film of sweat on mine. I quickly brushed it off on the side of my pants while I took in his round face and sloppy demeanor. His tie was crooked and poorly knotted on the top.

"Officer Ray," the tall suit said, shaking my hand. He held a firm grip without a trace of sweat, unlike his partner, and his tie was neatly done. "It's a pleasure to meet you. We've heard a lot about you and your agency. Pretty impressive."

"Thank you," I said, standing my ground. "We're pretty proud of ourselves. Life on the streets is a fairly tough business, you know."

Any good cop resents Internal Affairs. Their careers are based on political appointments and ratting on other officers, which is why they're referred to as the Rat Squad. They're not concerned with who is good or who is bad, just their own hides and rising to the top of the chain. That's a hard piece of crow to chew on when you're a civil servant, making minimal pay for a job where your life is on the line every day. The fact that someone like this can come along and question your motives, or the things you did to get your job done, and make you appear to be the bad guy when you're just doing what your country requested, is infuriating. The street comment was meant to hit a nerve.

"William, we're here to speak with you about Shep," the tall one stated. Clearly, that comment had worked as I intended.

"Okay," I said, still standing in the center of the office.

"We hear you have a great relationship with your ex-director. Is that correct?" the sloppy one asked.

"Had."

"Excuse me?" he responded.

"I *had* a great relationship with Shep. I haven't seen him since you guys pushed him out."

"Mmm, so you wouldn't have any knowledge of him working for the Native Americans then?"

"He wouldn't work for those bastards," I said, rolling off their question. "He's working for a company that ships products across the country."

That was a direct lie.

"You've got it wrong, Billy," the tall, stuffy one said, taking a step closer to me. "We have information that proves he's been working with the Native Americans. He's advising them on who the investigators are in our regions, telling them what vehicles they drive, along with the times and dates they're not there."

Sloppy Suit jumped in and began steamrolling me with all types of allegations. According to him, Shepard had been helping the Native Americans smuggle cigarettes via his pass, cleared by our stations, to go in and out of the reservation without cause for us to stop and search his vehicle.

"I'm sorry, guys, but I'm not buying it," I said. "Shep dedicated his life to this office and his work. To hear someone smear his character and attempt to put him in a dark light is pretty low, to be honest."

"The only person responsible for putting him in a dark light is Shep," Sloppy Suit said.

"Well, I'd like to say I had something for you boys that could prove otherwise, but other than the millions of dollars he brought to the state through his successful, closed cases, I'm afraid you've hit a dead end. Now, if you don't mind, I have some work to get to."

"Actually, we do mind," Tall Suit said, stepping in front of me. "We have a job to do as well, and we're going to need a bit more cooperation from you to successfully complete it."

"How's that?" I pondered out loud. But the second it was out of my mouth, I knew what they were going to ask me to do.

"We're going to need you to make a social call," Sloppy Suit said. "See how he's doing and if it gets anywhere."

"Sorry, guys, but I'm going to pass." I snickered. "Those are some serious suspicions you have against him, and to be blunt, I don't really care to be involved in it because I don't think they're true."

"A little birdie told us you might feel that way." Tall Suit smiled, pulling a sealed letter from his jacket pocket. "We had a bit more faith in you. However, not as much faith as our birdie, I guess."

The suit handed me a written order. I knew what it was

going to say before I even opened it, and sure enough, I was correct. It was a direct order demanding contact with Shep. If I disobeyed, I'd most likely be terminated.

Deep down, I still believed that Shep would never put our lives in danger. But the moment I picked up the phone, the suits happily watching me, I prayed I'd judged him correctly. I also prayed that Shep would be smart enough not to say anything the Rat Squad could use against him, especially while I was on the line.

I purposely dialed Shep's home phone, knowing there was only a five percent chance he'd be there. But per Murphy's Law, Shep picked up on the second ring.

"Shep, it's Billy," I said, my voice breaking as I attempted to catch my breath. I hadn't expected him to answer, and the shock sent my blood pressure through the roof.

"Hey, Billy! Long time, no hear. You still got that beautiful blonde around that I can come visit?"

He was referencing my wife, whom he'd met on several occasions. We'd gotten together with our wives a few times for dinner, but I didn't want the suits to know that. The more they knew how close Shep and I were, the more they'd be on my back.

"Somehow she's still around," I joked.

"I don't know how." Shep laughed. "You got real lucky with that one."

"And she's kind enough to remind me of that every day."

The Rat Squad began waving their hands in circles, gesturing for me to move the conversation along. I ignored them. The longer I made small talk, the longer it would give me to sort things out in my head.

But, of course, Shep, being the smartass that he was, foiled my plan and stepped directly into the shit I was trying to avoid.

"You hear about my new job?"

The suits sat upright.

"Yeah, unfortunately I did. I heard you're a lawyer again, out whoring yourself to all different types of companies."

"And good ones at that," he scoffed. "I'm sure you heard."

Shep's a smart man, so I was praying he'd caught on to this call. After all, he was probing, too. I could only pray the questions he was coaxing me to ask him were the ones that held the right answers. I couldn't be the one responsible for taking this man down. Not Shep.

"Actually, there are a few rumors going around that you're giving up information to the Native Americans about our vehicles and where we're stationing ourselves. I know that can't be true, Shep, but they're saying you're giving out the names and addresses of everyone who works here."

I held my breath, anxious for his response. *Please don't fuck yourself here*, my mind screamed. *Please don't be involved in this bullshit.*

"That's exactly why I left that snake pit, Billy. The character assassinations that go on just so people can step over you to get a better job—they're unbelievable. You think it's bad with the rank and file? It's ten times worse in the Ivory Tower. When I got up to take a piss, I'd get at least five or six knives in my back on the way to the urinal," he continued.

I tried to deter him and pull him away from the rant the IA guys were recording.

"I don't know, boss. I gotta admit the accusations flying

around are pretty strong." I sighed into the phone. "I was a little pissed when I heard some of them, especially because I know sometimes people mess up and do stupid things."

"Billy, you know me. You know I would never do that. I've spent too much of my life building what we worked for."

"I know, boss. That's why I wanted to give you a call. The shit they're saying isn't good. They're linking you to the Native Americans and taking what we worked for down with them."

"Even though I hate most people in the Ivory Tower, I would never give up any information that would put anyone in danger, and they know that. Plus, as devious of a bastard as you are, I know that once I left, you changed all the tactile operations. Anyone insinuating I could know that information wouldn't be targeting just me, they'd be targeting you as well, Billy. Be careful."

My ears went hot.

"If anything was smuggled, I would hear about it after the fact. Plus, I respect all you guys out there. If I knew anything, you'd be the first person I'd reach out to. I'm just a lawyer for whatever situation they, or anyone else, needs me for. It's a legality anyone can happily look up if they'd like to push further."

The agents next to me began shifting in their chairs, irritated.

"I never doubted you for a second, Shep. But you know how sticky things can get around here."

The suits flagged their hands back and forth like traffic cops. They didn't want me to end the call.

"You know what we should do, Billy?" Shep continued,

despite my attempt to wrap up the conversation. "We should go public with the details of what it takes to make a case work under a political agenda. We could expose how everything happens, that as long as a politician gets a pat on the back, we can run with any operation we like. No pat on the back and the case suddenly isn't worth it, even if it's infringing on American laws. You think people would be interested in reading that, Billy?"

"I'm sure you'd get a few raised eyebrows," I said, glancing at the suits, who were turning red. "Listen, stay clean out there and try to report back every now and then. We don't want people thinking you're fully converted now."

"Wouldn't they love that?" Shep laughed. "That would be the next thing they'd be paying the press to run a story on, me in full Native American garb."

"You really can't wait to get yourself in trouble," I said.

"I've been in trouble since the day I walked into that job. They had me labeled. They wanted a smart man to deliver. Only they got nervous at how quickly I did what they asked and backed down. Can't have the man underneath you know more than you, right? That's their theory, isn't it?"

"I don't know about that," I said. Tall Suit's dark beady eyes were staring a hole through me.

"Billy, I want you to play it safe out there. They've got their puppeteers pulling all the right strings. Be careful what you do and stay safe."

Click.

"Who told you to hang up?" Tall Suit yelled before the phone left my hand. "You were supposed to keep him on longer. He was talking. You cut him off. Why?"

"Is it because you forewarned him?" Sloppy Suit questioned.

"Forewarned? I didn't know you were fucking coming here. How the fuck can I forewarn someone when I don't know something's happening?"

"You know more than you're letting on." Tall Suit sneered.

"This is why people don't respect you," I retorted. "You're not intelligent enough to figure it out."

The anger I felt over their accusations, and over what I'd just been forced to do, began to swell.

"My best guess is that you're the only two who knew you were coming here, other than your boss," I said, pointing my finger. "If Shep was forewarned, then the fucking rat you're looking for resides in your department."

Both suits' cheeks flushed red. I was making them angry, but as I've said before, anger is the perfect opportunity to get the response you need. I pulled the handheld recorder, which was still running, toward me and spoke into it clearly.

"If memory serves me correctly, your boss filed a sexual harassment case against Shep a few years back," I said. "That case was never found to be true. That leads me to believe this whole gig, which is being constructed from Director Barris's end, is a tad suspicious. She wanted him out so she could place someone else in his position. But that wasn't good enough. Now she wants to destroy his name. Maybe that's because your boss is keen on going after someone who caught her in a lie. She has to make herself look good again, right? But then I have to ask myself why the two of you would be so inclined to drag another hardworking detective's name through the mud. Is it because you feel like big, powerful men up there with your little suits and desk jobs? You've never had to work the streets. You've never known the emotions that come with raising your gun in pursuit, praying it's them before you. Your hardest job is uncovering information and running back to tell your boss before the next guy, like a bunch of women at a tea party. Hard line of work you've got there."

If Tall Suit had enough balls, he would have jumped over the desk and attacked me, but he didn't. It wasn't in his professional nature. Instead, he just decided to hit me where it hurt.

"Okay, Billy, if you're not tipping Shep off, you'll have no problem allowing us to monitor all of your calls," he stated.

"You'll also be willing to record all of your calls from Shep, even when you're outside of the office," Sloppy Suit added, grinning.

This wasn't an offer. It was a demand. The suits were letting me know, in a professional asshole type of way, that all of my phones and equipment would now be bugged. I could choose to sit here and watch them do it, or could choose to face their team of higher-ups for possible termination if I refused.

"Of course I wouldn't." I smiled. "But I'm sure you won't mind setting it up while I get back to work. I'd hate to think your boss is paying me to sit here and play chitchat with you two cowards all day. Feel free to brush some of the dust off my desk while you're setting up your shit, by the way. Unlike yours, my desk rarely gets used."

I plopped down in my office chair and began entering case files into the computer while they worked. I took my time, purposely typing with one finger, just to annoy them and so they had to work around me longer. And I must admit, watching them crawl under my desk did give me some satisfaction. I was tempted to let my boot slip into Tall Suit's ribs as he set up the wires under my desk, but I knew I needed to play it smarter. I also knew that I needed to find a way to speak to Shep on my own. I needed to hear what was going on. As a senior investigator who'd been diligently working on detecting smuggling for the past few years, I knew that not everything was traceable. There's always an escape route, if you will. All you have to do is sit back and find your way to it. And, within the time it took for the suits to set up their equipment, I'd already found mine.

The next morning, I brought Chad into my bugged office. Chad and I had worked together for some time. He was young, eager, and dying to get his teeth into something big since he'd been in the middle of a stagnant case for months. As a six foot five, three hundred pound Black man, Chad stood out, to say the least. His size and color prevented him from working any close up undercover cases, as the Native Americans and other folks up in North Country assumed people from various races came from the prison a few miles away. This thinking often shut down any attempt Chad would have made to get inside before he even got started.

"Listen up," I said as Chad walked into my office. "There's a car allegedly full of untaxed cigarettes coming from St. Regis and heading down the Northway toward Albany. I want you to follow it, regardless of how far it goes, and see where it stops. There's a chance it's heading down to the city, but we can't be certain. I need you to be prepared for a possible all-nighter."

Chad, who was one of my most trusted investigators and one of Shep's close allies, looked at me questioningly. I furrowed my brow and held my finger to my lips, signaling that someone was listening.

"Car 530 is available for you, but it needs filling up. I want you to head down to King's Market on Route 291. They've got the cheapest fuel price right now."

"Kings Market is out of the way," Chad tried to break in.

"No matter. It's cheaper, and we're trying to keep costs down," I said, waving my hands toward the ceiling like a lunatic. I was never good at charades.

"Whatever you say, boss," Chad spoke into the air sarcastically.

As Chad exited my office, I kept my eyes laser focused on his departure. Then I made a few routine calls, and assigned officers for new case leads. Once Chad left the building, I slowly gathered my things and told my secretary I was headed to the corner for a bite. My company vehicle was waiting in the garage, but I didn't trust it. In fact, I'd become so paranoid about what was bugged that taking a shower felt invasive.

I hopped into my car, checked my rearview for following cars, and rushed down to King's Market. My timing was impeccable. I pulled up alongside Chad just as he was about to drive off. I angled my front end to block his exit and signaled for him to roll down his passenger window.

"Due to the fact that you'll lose the vehicle you're about to pursue, why don't you stop and say hi to Shep on your way home?" I yelled through the car windows.

Chad was confused.

"Billy, what the fuck is going on? You got early onset of dementia or something? What the hell are you doing here?"

"Find Shep. Tell him Internal Affairs is looking into his

case and is currently trying to set him up. They're recording all his phone calls and have bugged the Plattsburg office."

"Wait, hold on," Chad said, attempting to process everything I was firing at him.

"There's no time to wait. I don't know if I have a tail or not, so we've got to be quick. You know where Shep's office is, correct?"

"Yeah, it's like two hours…"

"Listen to me. I want you to drive to the reservation and follow a vehicle. If a vehicle doesn't come out, then grab a room, book it with the company card, and wait. Grab a coffee. Let the cameras at the store see you. Then follow whatever car comes out, and when you're sure no one is watching you, depart for Shep's workplace and give him the message. Tell him what I just told you. Tell him I will be in touch once I can secure a line. If anyone sees you there, tell them you were in the area and wanted to say hello. Got it?"

"So I'm not really following any particular car?" he responded.

"Not unless you want to. Make it look clean and get the shit done. Shep's had our backs for too long for us to just let these bastards come in and destroy him. Until we know different or have reason to believe what they say is true, he's as clean as he's always been, as far as we care to know."

I watched as Chad pulled off. As far as I could tell, we'd covered our tracks well. But to be safe, I made sure to grab a bite to eat at the corner and went see a couple other investigators.

Two days later, Chad walked into my office and tossed a handwritten note on my desk.

"Sorry to let you down, boss." He smiled. "I lost the car along Route 12. I hung out and tried to track him, but it was unsuccessful. I put all my notes in the file."

I placed the note in my pocket and reprimanded Chad on his loss of the vehicle. I considered my performance Oscar-worthy, but Chad just threw an uncalled-for gesture my way.

I headed to the bathroom to open the note. It read:

Lake Placid. Tuesday. 2pm. Viewside Diner.

[2]
RUSTY

Shep was my first boss at PATB, and from where I'd come, he was a warm welcome. An entertaining guy from New York City, Shep had spent his life working up the ranks. He'd started his career as a police officer and later became a criminal lawyer. When it came to law and investigative shit, Shep had it nailed. He understood the system and, more importantly, knew how to play it just as well as everyone else. However, as smart as Shep was, he was also fucking nuts.

Raised with a fearless inhibition, Shep encouraged backhanded operations. Our position with the PATB was simple. We were to take down the smuggling operations that were coming across the Canadian border and into the United States via the Native Americans. What wasn't simple, however, were the rules and jurisdictions we had to work around in order to catch and eliminate those ongoing operations.

Fighting the war against the illegal activities of the Native Americans was something Shep was proud of. He'd boast about our operations and tell anyone within earshot that our team was what put our agency on top of the list.

While I was Shep's lead investigator by day, at night I became his "social director." If politicians or high-ranking officials were coming to check on us, my job was to arrange the evening's entertainment. I'd coordinate hotels and dinner reservations, and then Shep, who was already on the wild side, would take them to other locations I chose to remain ignorant about.

Shep was good at reading the big guys. If he knew they were the type who wanted to cut loose, he'd say, "Billy, do what you do." And for the straight-and-narrow guys, he'd say, "Billy, keep it cool," which meant no crazy shit.

It was well known that Shep and I had a close relationship. I'd secured our most efficient CI, I was closing operations left and right, and I was shutting down crime rings that had run for generations. All of that, and the fact that I related to Shep, made me close with him. While he tended to be a crazy son of a bitch who worried some people, I took to his wild nature and fed off it. He made long work days enjoyable.

As a result of our bond, Shep showed me how to manage my career and work up the ladder. In three years, I rose from Senior Investigator to *the* Senior Investigator who was managing all of the operations within Plattsburgh's PATB.

"You understand that agencies in Albany are looking at your small Upstate office to see what you're doing," Shep said over beers one night. "Don't let that shit get to your head, Billy. But understand what you're worth."

When I joined Shep's team, his crew had been working on the borders outside of Buffalo and Massena. They'd made a few dents here and there, but they'd yet to land anything significant, and the pressure to do so was weighing heavily on Shep. The state had a lot of faith in him. His education, street smarts, and quick wit made him their person of interest when they assigned him this position. By the time he brought me on, five months into a lukewarm operation, he was feeling the heat and was desperate to step it up.

For those unaware of the Native American stipulations and land claims, I can tell you stepping it up is tricky. New York State made a land agreement with the Native Americans back in 1700 that granted them some of the lands they'd been diligently pursuing. The land was split across New York in what we know as the Six Nations: the Cayuga Gayohkohnyoh, Mohawk Kahnai'kehaka, Oneida Onyota'aka, Onondaga Ononda'ge, Seneca Onondawahgah, and Tuscarora Ska:rure. With these came the removal of state laws. New York State no longer had jurisdiction on the reservations.

These land claims would have been simple had the Native Americans played it right. They got their land and freedom to build whatever empire they wanted, which sounds fair—until someone wants more.

For the Native Americans up near Massena, that something more involved one of the few unpatrolled borders of Canada. Under the Jay Treaty, which was passed in 1794, the Native Americans were legally permitted to cross freely along the St. Lawrence River and the 45th parallel. Without New York State police or patrol borders allowed on these reservations, the border quickly filled with criminal enterprises. And by the 1980s, they were happily smuggling anything they wanted into this country. Think all cocaine routes were coming in through Mexico? Try again.

At the time I joined the PATB, the government was spending an alarming rate of taxpayer money to uncover how all the drugs, guns, and various illegal contraband were coming in.

When the United States government finally discovered that the missing link had been under its nose the whole time, they made sure the public didn't catch wind of it. Why? Because alarming the country with the news that we'd basically given a group of individuals a legal contract to smuggle anything they wanted into our country, and we technically couldn't do jack about it, wouldn't make for a very good political agenda, now would it?

To quietly solve the problem, New York State developed a task force that operated under the law known as ATTEA. ATTEA was a class-action lawsuit from *New York State v. Milhem ATTEA Bros.* in 1994 where the United States Supreme Court brought forth an injunction against the Native Americans. In short, Native Americans were given the right to purchase untaxed cigarettes for their reservation and people. However, it was deemed illegal to sell them off the reservation. Seems like an easy case-closed situation, right? Yet, even with the law in hand, the Native Americans continued to receive 10,000 cases of cigarettes a week. That number was ambiguous. The Native Americans held a ballpark of 2,500 people living on reservations. Even if they sold ten cartons of cigarettes to each person, which would have to include children, they still wouldn't make a dent in sales in the five digits. Obviously, the numbers didn't add up. It became the task force's job to spearhead a campaign to find out what was happening with all these untaxed cigarettes. And guess who they brought on to oversee it? None other than good old Mr. Shep.

Our task force was a multi-unit team, which included the Drug Task Force, ICE (who worked to uncover illegal immigrations), and the Petroleum, Alcohol, and Tobacco Bureau. Why the PATB, you ask? Well, part of the illegal contraband they were smuggling included cigarettes, liquor, and motor fuel. While that might sound minimal, these untaxed items created a large deficit for New York State. And since the state needed money to make up for the loss it had created, and they really wanted to get the Native Americans, our agency was placed on board.

The PATB had been a fairly quiet unit. But with Shep now taking the lead, and New York State wanting to repair its ego, the PATB rose to an entirely new level. And boy was it heated.

When I walked into the unit, they hadn't seen activity for two months. They'd attempted to seize tractor trailers and crack down on a few operations, but each one had failed. Shep was growing angry, and the state was questioning his progress.

"Take down a fucking truck, goddamn it!" Shep screamed on my first day. "Everyone's just sitting out there with their fingers up their asses. We need something fucking quick or we're all out of a job. And I am not about to be the supervisor who gets the can because his investigators were lazy or chicken shit. Now, go!"

As per the land treaty, our unit was not allowed to set foot on the reservation. We were also not allowed to show force against the Native Americans. Imagine stopping a tractor trailer, without any weapons or use of force, and demanding they step out and open the trailer. It was laughable. Within minutes, we'd have hundreds of Native Americans coming off the reservation in defense of their cargo, and we'd have to back down.

During my first week on the job, our unit did manage to arrest two individuals who were transporting untaxed liquor. It was a tiny crumb compared to what was going on inside those Native American land borders, but for Shep, it showed initiative.

Another problem with our laughable takedowns was that, every time we tried to make an arrest, we had to wait another week and reposition ourselves before we could make a move. It was a hell of a lot of politics and red tape, which began to feel heavy on any investigator trying to do his job. For Shep, it made him think outside the box.

"If we can't fuck them, then it's time to fuck their buyers," Shep announced. "We're going to start watching who they're delivering to, and we're going to arrest them. It's time we started fighting fire with fire. They want to cockblock us every time. Well, let's cockblock every fucking business they've ever known and cut their funds off at the balls."

Shep had mapped out units for our investigators all across the Buffalo-Massena area. As soon as a truck pulled out, we'd follow it, watch where it unloaded, then step in and seize the illegal material they'd delivered and arrest the buyers. We didn't give a fuck if the Native Americans saw us or not. And we made sure to let every buyer know, as we handcuffed their crying asses, that their Native American friends had given them up.

When the Native Americans' business partners began to

catch on and tried to find different loopholes to sneak products in, we'd turn and search for the smallest cracks in the buyers' systems and arrest them. Code violation, tax slipups, underage liquor sale, littering. We booked their asses and rode them until they cut ties with the Native Americans altogether.

While the tactic was working, and New York State was praising Shep, this only forced the Native Americans to retreat to other areas. Crossing state lines turned the case into one politicians could really sink their teeth into. Soon enough, the government wanted more, and therefore so did we.

One day I strolled into Shep's office. "I've got a guy," I said.

"What kind of guy?"

"He's on the inside. Works directly with the Native Americans as a pirate driver."

"He's willing to work with us?" Shep questioned, his eyebrows burrowing into one another.

"He's pissed. They fucked him a few weeks back. A tribe member stole his Harley. Since the guy who stole it is protected by the Native American family, and he ain't, he's not getting shit back. So he called us. He's willing to tell us everything."

"Why the fuck did he call you?"

"We arrested him a few months back for untaxed motor fuel. He said I was nice to him, so he thought I'd help him out." I didn't bother to add that when I arrested him he was only wearing coveralls—no shirt and no underwear—which I knew because he stripped to show me he had no weapon on him!

Rusty, who was a low-key guy, around six foot two and

about one hundred ninety pounds, had asked for more than help. He wanted these guys to disband and crumble. For him, it would be the ultimate revenge, and I couldn't say I disagreed.

The Native Americans often hired pirate drivers like Rusty who were not of Native American descent and didn't reside on the reservations. That way, if a driver was caught, the Native Americans could claim innocence and lack of relations.

Rusty had been a pirate driver for the Native Americans for years. The evening we arrested him and impounded his tractor trailer, he'd remained aloof because he believed the Sovereign Nation would come to his aid. It was the same bull-shit story they'd fed to all of their outside business contacts. But, when Rusty was placed in a cell, where he sat for two days without a word from his trusty buddies, he began to question the stories he'd been told.

The way Rusty spoke, referring to me as "Officer Billy" and mispronouncing a few words, initially made me write him off as an uneducated hick. But it turned out this guy was pretty smart. Not only did he have names, locations, and secret truck routes, he'd been logging everything for almost ten years in case he ever needed backup. Now, thanks to the wonderful emotion of anger, he was ready to hand it all over.

This was our first big-ticket operation.

"If this guy is who he says, then we need his help," Shep said as he flipped through some files to find the informant paperwork. "But if he doesn't pull through, it's your ass, Billy. You okay with that?"

For whatever reason, I trusted Rusty. He was angry and spiteful, and I'd learned those emotions could get a person to say and do things their rational sense would otherwise disregard. If we had a chance of doing anything big, it had to be with Rusty on our side. If he didn't deliver, well, I was most likely sailing out of that position anyway.

"If you want my agency to work with you, you're going to have to show us something," I informed Rusty via phone. "My office isn't willing to work with you unless you've got something substantial to put on the table."

"I've got a gig going down next week," Rusty readily replied. "A large tanker of motor fuel is coming down from St. Regis to a place in Utica. I can supply documentation, tell you where it'll be positioned, and who the final buyer is."

We were in. Shepard immediately rounded up a team of guys and had us ready to go.

"You're the lead, Billy," Shep said, handing me the paperwork. "Don't fuck this up!"

I spent the next few days in a state of excitement, anticipation, and sheer anxiety. At times, I didn't know if I should map out more routes, on top of the twenty-five I'd already unnecessarily done, or treat myself to an overstuffed meatball sub and watch football. My mind was running a mile a minute with scenarios, good and bad, and the aftermath of what a successful—or unsuccessful—operation like this would do for our agency. Needless to say, I got very little sleep those next few days. However, by the day of the operation, my nerves had subsided. I was laser-focused and ready to tackle the first big lead in my career. The weather, however, had other ideas.

A huge storm hit Upstate New York the afternoon of my departure. Roads were covered in snow, highways were closing, and driving was ill-advised. But that, we learned, was for business professionals and uppity types. For bad guys delivering untaxed motor fuel on a strict timeline, bad weather simply meant fewer cops and informants to watch them. So, despite my team's apprehension and the condition of the thruway, which was already threatening to close, we stuffed ourselves in a mid-sized Ford Fusion and began our pursuit.

During an operation such as this, all investigators had to maintain a chain of evidence. That meant we had to have eyes on Rusty as he picked up the motor fuel from St. Regis, while he transported it across the highway, and when he signed the tanker over to the purchaser. But per Murphy's Law, anything that could go wrong did go wrong.

Our guys couldn't keep up with Rusty from the start. His tractor trailer was carrying a load of motor fuel, which made his vehicle heavier and therefore more able to plow through the snow-covered roads in a quicker fashion. We hadn't even been on the road for an hour and we'd already lost sight of him twice. Both times I had to call Rusty to tell him to slow down.

By the third call, Rusty was pissed.

"I'm on a time schedule. You gotta tell your guys to speed it up. I can't keep pulling over on the side of the highway to wait for them."

"You're driving a truck filled with motor fuel, you idiot. Slow the fuck down!"

"Your guys keep slowing me down and you won't have an operation to shut down, you understand? My guys will suspect something if I'm not on time, and they'll leave. They're not like you. They have other shit to do."

I tried to ease Rusty's irritation with a few jokes about New York State not being able to pay for all-wheel drive to ease him up a bit. But, by the time we reached our destination, thirty minutes after his anticipated arrival time, no joke could make up for what Rusty had predicted. The bad guys had left.

My heart was in my throat. I choked down the thought of calling my boss as I watched Rusty pound on the hood of his truck across the way.

"I'm sticking my neck out here, and you assholes are holding the machete!" Rusty yelled into the phone.

"Rusty, calm down. Call your guys and see where they are before we get all worked up."

Rusty flooded the line with a few inappropriate terms about my team's inadequacy and hung up.

We'd parked our unmarked vehicle across the street from him in a small alley that acted as a walkway between two large, empty factories. We were in direct view of his truck, so I watched as Rusty dialed numbers and paced around the parking lot, talking.

"They want me to sit tight," Rusty hammered back into the line. "That means you assholes are costing me money. You better fucking compensate me for this shit."

"Don't get worked up yet," I told him. "They'll be here, right?"

"Yes, they'll fucking be here so you can have your precious operation," he replied. "At least one of us gets something out of this shit. It sure as hell ain't me."

I didn't know what we could do for Rusty, but I needed him to remain calm and stay on the case. I couldn't have him leave. So I lied.

"The agency will cover your costs. Don't worry. We'll take care of you as long as you take care of us."

Truth be told, I didn't know if the agency could offer him squat. I could only pray they'd see what he was doing for us and be willing to provide him with some leverage.

The snow continued to fall as we waited in the alley. Two hours went by, and cars were nowhere to be seen. The roads were now blanketed in snow, and from what I could tell, the plows were inept at keeping up with the pace.

After another hour, one of our fellow investigators took on the dirty deed of marching up the road, through calf-high snow, and bringing back a fast food dinner.

"We got you a Big Mac," I told Rusty. "Ben left it by the bridge 'bout one hundred feet to your right."

"Thanks," Rusty said and hung up.

Pissed or not, we watched as he hopped out of his cab and walked to the assigned area to retrieve his dinner. The guys and I wolfed down our food and chatted well into the evening. But by the time midnight hit, our spirits were beginning to dwindle.

All three of us were considerably large guys. Brihiem was six foot one and about 185 pounds. George was six foot two and weighed in around 210. I was six foot one and around 200 pounds. Legroom quickly became an issue. We all felt the need to stretch out. However, with snow now reaching the tops of our calves, and none of us sporting boots high enough to prevent the snow from falling into our socks, the options began closing in by the hour.

By two a.m., it was clear we would be spending the night in the vehicle. We slept in shifts so we never lost eyes on the truck, and we used our coats to act as pillows and blankets. To save on gas, we had to turn the car off for as long as we could withstand the plummeting temperatures that crept into the vehicle.

For two days, our crew continued to sit tight. We were restless, exhausted, and quick to jump at any car that turned down the secluded street. We were living off fast food and gas station coffee, and our lack of showers had permeated the car.

"You gotta call your guys again," I pleaded into the phone. "My guys are getting edgy, and frankly so am I."

Rusty told us his guys were being cautious.

"They've got eyes on this tanker just as much as you do right now." He sighed.

For that reason, we didn't dare make any sudden movements. Rusty reassured us that his employer had told him to stay put.

"It's what I fucking told you," Rusty said happily into the line. "They're fucking suspicious because I was late. I'm never fucking late."

"It was a fucking blizzard!" I yelled into the phone, irritated and now a tad anxious about my job. "Don't these assholes watch the Weather Channel or look outside their fucking window?"

"No." Rusty chuckled. "They're criminals. A job is a fucking job—especially when it reaps a heavy reward."

For forty-nine hours, we sat inside our fermenting vehicle, waiting. The chatter had long died down, and the snow outside was beginning to melt. The street had been plowed, making the black pavement now shine with wet puddles, and people had sprung from their quiet hibernation and were milling around. My guys and I were growing delirious.

"So, Billy, what do you think you'll do when they fire you from this job?" George asked.

"Well," I said, running my hands over my rough, unshaven face, "I'm guessing the first thing I'll do is find the asshole who was supposed to be behind the rig pickup and kick his ass."

"If you're planning on getting fired, why don't we just find the asshole now and get it over with?" Brihiem interjected from the backseat.

"Just a little bit longer, guys." I sighed, tired of listening to the whining. I wanted out of the car and away from them just as much as they wanted out and away from me. "There's no way they're just going to let this load drop. There's too much money at stake. Someone will come to claim it."

"They better come to claim it soon," Brihiem whined again. "My back is in knots, and I can't eat another hamburger. I haven't taken a shit in two days. That junk has me all backed up."

I turned my head back to the movement on the street. The thought of Brihiem's bowels and our less-than-decent meals heightened my anxiety. I needed to get out of the car, needed to be away from these people and their mindless conversations.

"I'm going to stretch my legs for a minute," I said, opening the car door.

The yellow river of piss we'd created over the past two days was currently being washed away by the melting snow. Still, I made myself useful, adding another stream to the pile, just to entertain myself. I began to think about the length of time it would take for my newly added layer to wash away.

I should probably check every fifteen minutes, I reasoned

inside my head. *Every fifteen minutes, I can see how quickly the snow is melting.*

I paced up and down the alleyway, looking at the side of the now-empty warehouses, wondering what life inside must have been like. I studied the details of the rounded windowpanes, the wooden doors, the thick, heavy handles, and the locks. I began contemplating how I could break into the building. How easy it would be. How safe.

As I walked further down the alley, surveying the height and number of windows on the floor above me, Brihiem shouted my name.

"He called!" Brihiem yelled from the window of the car, too whiny to open the door and step out. "They're on their way!"

My whole body immediately woke from its haze and began hauling toward the car.

"What do you have?" I questioned, my breathing heavy from the mini-sprint I'd just done.

"They'll be here in ten was all he said."

"Okay," I said, straightening myself back in my seat. "This is it. Let's not fuck it up."

Brihiem focused his camera, while George and I stared down opposite ends of the street, unsure which direction the truck would be approaching from.

Then, finally, after forty-nine long hours, a large black rig turned onto the street from the west.

My crew and I sat up, full of anticipation. The excitement in my body was unlike any high I'd ever felt before. My left leg began to bounce up and down as we watched the truck pull into the lot beside Rusty. Our standoff was about to officially pay off. The bad guys had come to claim their tanker.

Rusty quickly dialed my number and left it open so that my team and I could record the conversation. Being that our operation wasn't the highest of ends, we had to use a handheld recorder, which George held up to my phone. I turned on the speaker and watched as Rusty slowly approached the short, stocky man who had gotten out of the truck.

We listened in as this man apologized to Rusty. Believe it or not, the man had gotten into a fight with his wife and had spent the last two days on a bender. A fucking bender! Here we'd been stuffed in a car for two days, freezing our asses off and constipating Brihiem, while this asshole was in a bar downtown having a grand old time.

The short asshole begged Rusty not to report him to his boss.

"This is the second time I've fucked up," he said, another whiner on the scene. "This will be it for me."

"Just sign for the shit so I can get the hell out of here, buddy. I've been living in that truck for two fucking days!" Rusty exclaimed.

"Right, of course," the asshole spit out.

We watched as he reached into his jacket pocket and pulled out a white envelope filled with cash.

"You don't mind if I count it, right? I mean, at this point I don't think a dog would trust you."

"No, no. Go ahead," the short asshole said.

Rusty counted $20,000 out loud so we could capture every dollar on tape. He also stood to the side, raising the bills just high enough out of the envelope so Bryan could snap the pictures without Shorty getting suspicious.

"Good thing it's all here," Rusty said, placing the envelope inside his jacket pocket. "Pull your rig closer so I can get the fuck out of here."

In under ten minutes, Rusty had taken the money from the buyer, transferred the motor fuel, and driven away.

Our job with Rusty was done, so we let him depart the scene and head home, free and clear of our slow vehicles, while we stayed behind to follow the tanker. To our surprise, the asshole delivered the fuel to a gas station just eight-tenths of a mile down the road. Talk about stupid!

Brihiem recorded the stocky asshole shaking hands with a taller gentleman who had walked out, checked out the rig, and gestured to his fuel tanks. It was the asshole's job to transfer the fuel into his pumps, so we waited for him to set up his equipment, place the transfer nozzle into the gas station's tank, and then, in my first glorious moment as an investigator, we swarmed the tanker like wild banshees.

The short asshole had no idea what was happening as we sped up to the scene, our lights blazing, and jumped out of the car like we were on a TV show. George ran inside to seize the tall gentleman, while I went straight for the short asshole.

"Good morning, Asshole," I said, my gun drawn. "Mind stepping toward me?"

The asshole hesitated for a second, looking wildly around. My heart leaped at the thought of him running. My legs and body were so stiff I'd barely made it back to the car moments ago. If he ran, I wouldn't be able to keep up.

"WALK TOWARD ME NOW!" I shouted, hoping to eliminate any thoughts he was having of trying to flee.

Reluctantly, the asshole took his hands from the pump, placed them in the air, and slowly walked toward me. I grabbed his arms and swung him around to cuff him behind his back.

"You're under arrest for the transportation of untaxed motor fuel," I said, listing his rights.

To my surprise, the asshole started to cry.

"Shit just ain't going right anymore," he said. "It just ain't going right."

I pulled him over to our vehicle, which was now filled with fast food wrappers and two days' worth of old coffee, just as George and Brihiem walked over with the tall gentleman in cuffs.

"It's your lucky day, boys," I said as they approached.

"Fuck you," the tall gentleman spat. His hair was growing thin on top, and his teeth were brownish-yellow.

"I'm not talking to you, Baldy." I laughed. "I'm talking to the fine investigators who just helped arrest you. I'm going to buy them coffee on our way home."

Baldy hung his head down as we placed him inside our cramped, smelly vehicle beside his asshole friend. Brihiem slid in beside them, and we pulled away—happy to be riding in our car instead of living in it.

"We're gonna need to get some gas soon," George replied as he started the car.

"You don't mind if you fuel our tank up, do you there, Baldy?" I asked, positioning my visor mirror to look at him.

"Not a fucking bit," he grunted.

"Ah, that's the spirit, Baldy," I said, smiling back at him.

We pulled up to the pumps, filled our tank to the brim, and drove the assholes to the station for booking. We'd successfully made the first large arrest for our agency, and I can't express how good that felt.

After the arrest, Shep began the official process to make Rusty our agency's official Confidential Informant. His title was now CI-111-PL. He was exclusive to us, and his identity was known to only a few members on our team. Shep worked hard to maintain that and would go on to risk his job for Rusty's sake a few years down the road. Yet, ironically, the man who saved our agency, the man who Shep would sacrifice his career for, would be the man responsible for taking him down.

[3]
SHEP BEING SHEP

For the rest of that week, I buried myself in my work to try to keep my mind from reading into my meeting with Internal Affairs and Shep's so-called involvement. Diving into my work brought up an interesting event. McNamara, the senior investigator of a sister agency in Lake Placid, had attempted to bring me out there for weeks. Scheduling a meeting with him the morning of the Shep meet-up was the perfect way to cover my ass. So come Tuesday, I wrapped up my morning cases and drove to the Lake Placid office for a twelve p.m. meeting. McNamara was waiting for me as I shuffled through the doors.

"Billy," he called out as he walked over to me and shook my hand. "It's been a while."

"Aw, we've been busy, guy," I replied, following him into his office. "You know how it is. I'm glad I was able to get out here today."

"As are we," McNamara said, gesturing for me to take a seat beside the small coffee table in his office.

As a shorter fellow, McNamara rang in around five foot nine and 170 pounds. He ran a fairly successful office but had never really caught any big fish, so to speak. Our offices had worked together from time to time. We'd collect information and discuss smuggling operations. And since bad guys tended to move around, we'd cover what cases intersected with each other.

McNamara was a stand-up guy. He was always out for his agency's win but wasn't willing to cut corners or play dirty, like the rest of us. His goal was to create a solid foundation that investigators could continue to build upon. So much of his time was spent playing with numbers and scenarios. He was what we referred to as a fact man. I knew going out there, per his continual invitations, he had something new he wanted to run by me. My only hope was that his pitch would last long enough to carry me into one thirty yet short enough to end by one forty-five.

"Again, thank you for coming out here today," McNamara said, placing a cup of black coffee in front of me. "I have something I've been working on that I think could really benefit all of our agencies."

"One day your mind is going to get tired of your theories and shut down," I teased him. "We're going to find you sitting by a ditch slurping mud."

"As my wife tells me." He laughed. "But for now, I'm insistent on pushing through."

McNamara pulled out a bunch of manila folders and spread them across the miniature table between us.

"I've taken the time to map out every one of our jurisdictions, and I've seen how some of our paths might strengthen one another," McNamara explained, referencing three different large maps, all covered with red *X* marks, agency names, and Native American entrance and exit routes.

"If we all band together, I think we can produce an unbreakable chain that will break down the Native Americans' whole operation in under six months," McNamara continued.

"You mean like some Hands Across America shit?" I questioned.

"Not to that extent," McNamara said, rising from his seat and hanging the maps beside his whiteboard, which was full of numbers, names, and descriptions I couldn't grasp. "I've located some alternative routes that I think the Native Americans are utilizing. Each route leads to a cut-off extension that runs into another agency's jurisdiction. I'm thinking, if we can get everyone on board, we can cut them off on both points, inevitably closing the routes they've been utilizing for years."

"That sounds interesting," I said. "What other agencies do you have on board so far?"

"None." McNamara smiled. "I knew I had to sell you first. If I can get your agency on board, I know the rest will follow."

"So I'm your platform, so to speak."

"Not a platform, Billy," McNamara said, flipping over another map. "A key. People respect you and look to your agency for guidance in all that you've done. If I can sell you this idea and get you to work with us, everyone else will simply follow. You'd be the ringleader that gets this operation off the ground. You'd reap all the success."

"Well, unfortunately, I'm learning that success comes with an awful lot of strings, not all pleasant, I might add."

"We've heard." McNamara shrugged. "But who cares? If you have something that can change everyone's perspective and can shut down any remaining gossip that's out there, then why not take a chance and go for it?"

For a diversion, McNamara's meet-up was beginning to show promise.

"What have the bosses said about this?" I inquired.

"I haven't run it by them, either." McNamara sighed.

I couldn't help but laugh. For a numbers guy, McNamara was way off on this one.

"Why the laughter?" McNamara questioned. "You don't think they'll go for it?"

"Not if I'm on board." I snickered. "If you approach the bosses with my agency's name on the top of your list, you better plan on saying adios to what you've got going."

Despite myself, I told McNamara a quick summary of what was going down: Shep leaving, Shep possibly working for the other side, our agency being questioned.

"That can't be right," McNamara stated. "I've worked with Shep for years. And your agency, they practically disbanded an underground operation the government hadn't been able to touch. You guys are legends to the other agencies. Everyone's trying to do what you guys did."

"Well, I thank you for that." I sighed. "It's been a rough go for the past few months. But I will definitely look into your proposal and think about it some more."

"I appreciate that, Billy."

"One thing. When you do go to the bosses with this, make sure you leave our name for last. I think you've got something here, and I'd hate for our agency to be the reason you didn't get a chance to put this together in your career."

I lingered around McNamara's office for another twenty minutes, pretending to study his maps and outlines, when I was actually just looking to add extra time.

I SPENT THE FIFTEEN-MINUTE DRIVE TO THE DINER thinking about Shep and McNamara. I'd forgotten how close they were and how often Shep had sought out his expertise on cases and positioning. By the time I pulled into the parking lot of the rundown meeting point, I'd committed to the fact that, regardless of what was going on with Shep, I was going to contact McNamara and sign onto his operation. If anything, working with another intelligent investigator might be just what we needed to get my agency, and myself, out of the mess we'd found ourselves in.

I put the car in park, immediately understanding Shep's location of choice. Despite its desolate surroundings, the diner, which was set inside an old trailer, sat back from the street at an angle, making it easy to see approaching traffic from all sides. The crunch of old rocks echoed underneath my boots as I walked across the dirt lot and up two wooden steps to the screen door. As I stepped inside, the old door squeaking behind me, I saw Shep, nestled in the far back corner, smiling at me. He looked more casual than I'd seen him in years. His usually groomed haircut had grown out a bit, and he'd traded his typical polo shirts for a Syracuse sweatshirt and jeans.

"Those dumb bastards." Shep laughed as he stood up to give me a hearty handshake and slap on the back. "I knew everything, Billy. I knew they'd come after me from the start. Despite what they think, I still have a lot of friends in the Ivory Tower. I was waiting for your call days before you rang. Those lazy bastards sure took their time."

"You knew I would be calling?" I questioned, taking a seat across from Shep.

"Of course I knew." He smiled. "I'm not that far out of the loop yet. Those bastards can't keep their mouths shut for shit."

"Why the hell did you answer the phone, then?"

"Because I had to break their balls, Billy. You know just as well as I do that this is a sham. I'm their scapegoat. They can't get shit done because they don't give their guys the right tools or the respect and confidence to get it done. They're too busy documenting everyone's steps because they're too fucking scared to do anything. Instead, they do nothing at all. But they don't see that. What they see are answers. Answers that they need to provide to their bosses. Meet their answer." Shep smiled, his arms extended.

"Stop fucking smiling," I said, annoyed. "This is serious. They've got charges pending against you. They're listing you as a conspirator and laying claim that you're giving up information."

"Oh, please. I'm not worried about them. They won't find out shit because I'm not doing shit. I'm a lawyer, point blank. People hire me from all over. Turning someone away doesn't give me any merit."

"It does if you spent three years trying to tear them down."

"Ah, but that's where you're wrong. I don't deal in their smuggling ring, as the bosses would like everyone to believe. I'm a lawyer for land and state tax violations. Theoretically, as much as we're trying to uncover their illegal smuggling operations, we're breaking the New York state law of ground protection by bringing undercover officers on their land. The Native Americans don't know that, but I do."

"I still don't get how you would want to do that. We fought to get under contract for that. *You* helped us fight for that, and now you're the one going after the person who you swayed to approve it."

"If you're asking if that's the same person who was behind the inquiries and lies about my character, then yes, that's the same person I'm going after," Shep stated coldly. "An eye for an eye, right, Billy?"

I sat there staring at Shep in disbelief. His switch had nothing to do with the other side. It had everything to do with revenge.

"I was wrong in what I did and what I had the agency agree to do. I was caught up in the job, but that was my boss' responsibility to see that. And he didn't. He signed forms and gave us permission to do whatever the fuck we wanted, as long as it meant closed cases and money for him to take to his bosses."

"So help me understand," I said, running my fingers through my hair. "You're helping the Native Americans fight a case against the state based on land claims you got them to sign."

"Billy, we took down every fucking smuggling ring we

could and were successful. You know that. We never needed a signed document to sneak on their land. We did our shit outside of their reservation. All I ask is that the government respect that and stop trying to do things the easy way."

I sat there quietly listening to Shep. Did I think he was helping them? No. Did I think he was angry with the state and trying his best to fuck them? One hundred percent yes.

"It's one more reason why they need you and others to find anything you can to bring me down. They have nothing to build their case on besides my vehicle being on the reservation. Meanwhile, I have everything I need that can nail them to the full extent of the law. They're shitting themselves right now, Billy. And I have to admit, I'm liking it."

An older waitress arrived and placed a Southwest omelet in front of Shep and a double cheeseburger in front of me.

"I remembered," Shep said, gesturing to the lunch he'd taken the liberty of ordering. "I know my guys inside and out, Billy. I've taken care of you and always put everyone's safety first. I'm not willing to let them attack that."

"I do like them stacked and greasy." I smiled, loading condiments onto the burger. "And as for your guys, I don't think you have to worry about your character. They know how good you were to them and what you did for us. Right now, I think they're just confused as to what you're doing, but when it comes down to it, they can never say you were a bad boss."

"Does that mean you're ready to quit that shit job and come work for me again?" Shep grinned.

"I'm not a lawyer, Shep. You know that," I said, biting into my burger.

"You could be my driver. There'd be other duties, of

course, but I'd let you in on those once you got a look around—as a welcomed guest this time, that is."

I wiped the grease from my chin.

"God bless ya, Shep, but I could never work for the other side. Not after all I've seen and done."

"I understand," Shep said, salting his omelet. "But you understand that, even if you don't work for me, just helping me right now, and not helping Internal Affairs, is going to cost you, right? They aren't going to make your life easy."

"I guess that's the name of the game, though. We help them, they fuck us," I said, trying a fry.

By the time we departed, I felt confident that our meeting hadn't been in vain. Shep wasn't against us. He wasn't working for the Native Americans or giving up our intel. He was simply Shep being crazy and out to screw anyone who stood in his way.

I glanced in my rearview mirror and caught one last glimpse of Shep. I'd go on to hear about some of his endeavors over the next few years, but this would be the last time we'd see each other in person. He was right about one thing, though. Staying loyal to Shep was going to cost me. And I was about to feel that wrath faster than I'd expected.

Over the next three months, I didn't receive one phone call from Shep. If I called him, as directed, it would go straight to voicemail, or he'd answer, shoot the shit for five minutes, and hang up, claiming a client was coming in.

As for my agency, things were good. My team was in the

middle of a new case regarding a large number of untaxed goods coming across the Canadian border, the project with McNamara was gaining momentum, and the holidays had rolled in, which had everyone in an uplifted mood. But, while things seemed to be going well on our end, Internal Affairs wasn't having that great of a time. Their lives currently revolved around an end-of-the-year wrap-up, which meant it was time for them to speed up their incrimination of Shep.

One week after New Year's, my fine suit friends stopped in for another visit. Only this time they weren't as patient and friendly as before. I was in the field, directing my crew on the new shipment that was due to come off the reservation in two days, when my secretary Bobby called me.

"Your friends from Internal Affairs are here requesting your presence."

My whole body shrank with the sound of that name.

"What do they want?" I sighed, looking at the team of investigators waiting for me to deliver the final plans.

"You," Bobby said. "I told them to wait in the lobby, but they went straight into your office. It's not sounding too good in there."

"Fuck!" I yelled. "Tell the pricks to give me ten minutes."

I apologized to my crew.

"Keep your phones on," I said, walking to my car. "We'll meet back here as soon as this mess is cleaned up."

I walked into my office to find the suits waiting for me in a sea of shit. They'd emptied my desk, knocked over a filing cabinet, and torn my books from the shelves.

"Well, it looks like you gentlemen have been busy," I said,

stepping over the paperwork that covered the ground like a plush carpet. "Find something good in there, I hope?"

"You fucking tipped him off, you twisted bastard," Tall Suit spat as I walked toward my desk.

"Whoa, Suit Boys," I said, taking a seat. "Rough holiday? Santa not bring you what you want?"

"Enough with the bullshit!" Tall Suit shouted as he lunged toward my desk. "How the fuck did you tell him we were watching him?"

"Boys, I don't know what type of coffee you had this morning, but clearly you need to take it down a level. Maybe a.m. brew is more your speed."

"We're done dicking around here, William," Sloppy Suit said, shutting my office door.

"Thank God someone is." I smiled, leaning forward in my chair. If Sloppy Suit thought he was going to intimidate me, he was wrong. "I was nervous I was going to have to explain what we do in this office."

The suits frowned in confusion.

"Work," I enunciated. "We work here, and you boys are slowing down the movement."

"Listen, asshole," Tall Suit sneered, a ball of white spit forming in the corner of his mouth. "We know Shep was calling this office at least two times a week. Now he doesn't call once. That's reason enough for us to file charges."

"File charges based on what? That someone hasn't called me? You guys really are desperate, aren't you?"

"It depends on your meaning of desperate. If it's us seizing this office and shutting down all operations because we feel that you and your guys are assisting Shep in his new role, then yeah, we're that desperate."

Tall Suit crossed his arms over his chest and leaned back, smiling. He was clearly proud of himself and waiting for my horrified reaction. But he didn't know me that well.

"Guys, I did everything you asked." I sighed. "You forced me to bug my phone, you pushed me to call him, and you've monitored every call that's come in here, regardless if I was speaking with Shepard or not. You've got nothing. And you know how I know? Because I did nothing. If there is a leak, then it is in your office. But that shouldn't surprise you because all of your office has leaks, doesn't it?"

Tall Suit smiled. "Is that your final statement?" he asked.

"Other than your office is full of rats and you should be looking inside your infested walls for the leak instead of here where you haven't even found one dropping? Yeah, I think I'm good."

"Then I guess we're good here, too." Sloppy Suit smiled. "We'll be needing your computers and everyone's personal cell phones before we leave."

"Can you boys show me your papers?" I inquired, standing up from my chair.

Tall Suit handed me a warrant requesting my computer and personal cell. I tossed my phone onto the desk.

"Anything else?" I questioned. "Other than the fact that you won't be taking anything that belongs to my employees. That was a nice try, though."

Tall Suit smirked and nudged past me, pushing his way over to my computer. I had every intention of tripping him, but I let him by.

"I do have one final statement for you, though," I said to Sloppy Suit, who was still blocking my door. "You have shit taste in ties. My wife is a pretty generous woman and wouldn't mind taking your wife shopping. She can show her a thing or two, and maybe even show her how to help you tie your tie properly, you sloppy bastard."

Sloppy Suit took a step away from the door and walked toward me.

"You really are an asshole," he sneered, inches away from my face.

"You know what they say about assholes, right?" I smiled, looking down at his little stature. "Takes one to know one."

Sloppy Suit tilted his head to look up at me, and I laughed in his reddening face.

"As much as I'd like to chat, I have real people to imprison," I said, nudging past Sloppy Suit. He took a few steps back to catch himself. "Good luck on your future voyages, though. Can't wait to see what good cop you turn on next."

Before the suits could answer, I walked out, slamming the door behind me. For as much as I cared to know, those assholes would be busy trying to sweep a computer I barely knew how to use. That gave me a sense of amusement as I walked out of the office and headed back to my guys on the field. But, smile as I might, the suits would deliver another blow shortly.

"Reasonable doubt" allowed our tractor trailer, carrying thousands of dollars of untaxed items, to successfully cross the border while we stood by and watched. My team was enraged. They wanted to go public and leak the story to the press. But I knew a story like this would only fuel Internal Affairs, as well as the bad guys. An agency at odds was exactly what criminals needed to take charge. And Internal Affairs had played right into that scenario.

Overnight our team went from one of the top units in the agency to one that was broken. Despite our acting supervisor, a quiet gentleman the higher-ups had appointed as a temporary fill-in, the powers that be now enlisted the help of Lt. Booth and Assistant Investigative Director Post. I had history with Booth. Two years prior to Shep's departure, Booth and I had taken the test for an open chief position. I'd scored number one, while Booth failed to pass. However, when it came time to take the position, I opted to stay where I was. Booth called me at work to question my reasons for not taking the position.

"I'm not a desk guy," I said. "My heart lies in the field. So, for now, I'd like to stay here and see how far I can take it."

Booth gave me some bullshit praise before delivering his kicker. The only way he could receive an option for the position was if I signed off. If I had known what an asshole Booth would turn out to be, I would have laughed at his request and hung up on the bastard. But, at the time, I saw no need to hesitate, so I signed off—essentially helping Booth become the chief.

Within months, Booth became known for being one of the largest pricks in the agency. People left positions and revamped their schedules just to avoid him. For reasons unknown to me, Booth grew to despise my name. I believe I represented a dark secret that Booth hoped to keep in its cave. And, while I'd never thought to share his incompetence since I was busy in my own career, my very presence to Booth seemed to threaten his demise.

Post, on the other hand, had spent his entire career in New York City and hated everything about Upstate. He saw his additional gig here as a smack in the face and had a bitter taste for anyone who dared to work in this office.

Together the duo was one of the most brutal pairs since Lenin and Trotsky. They were both out for blood, and Internal Affairs was happy enough to paint it all over me.

Within a week of their takeover, my work vehicle was no longer available for personal use, something that had been agreed upon at the date of my hire, and all my ongoing investigations and authority were dismissed. My investigators had been disbanded and sent to different areas on small, insignificant jobs, while I was assigned to inspect small mom-and-pop stores in our four-county region, which included St. Lawrence, Franklin, Clinton, and Essex. I was to work by myself and complete seven inspections a day. My title no longer mattered, nor did the weather, how far I had to drive, or any logistical concerns. I was to complete seven inspections a day or face questioning.

And as for the personal use of my vehicle, well, let's just say it made the next year a living hell. Without a vehicle to drive back and forth to work, I was forced to ask fellow investigators for rides to and from the train station or, when times were rough, I'd catch a ride with a patrolman and hop from barrack to barrack until I made it home.

While I spent my days in punishment, Shepard was in and out of court due to charges placed on him by Internal Affairs. I'd catch wind of the latest court proceedings and try to decipher what his next move would be. I spent a lot of time focusing on his case. It was all I could do to drag myself out of my misery and tell myself to grin and bear it. Shepard was a smart lawyer with a grand criminal team behind him. If I were to be drawn up on charges, I wouldn't be as lucky.

[4]
LESSON LEARNED EARLY

Sometime early in my career while working on the Canadian border with my partner Barb Payne, we pulled over a motor fuel truck with no motor fuel placard identifying what was in the tanks.

We both approached the vehicle and identified ourselves as police officers, though we hoped that the red lights flashing on our vehicle and badges and guns exposed in plain view would make that somewhat obvious. But wearing plainclothes, you never knew.

I knew the incident could become complicated very quickly, because the vehicle was within a mile of the St. Regis reservation and the vehicle stop would result in crowds forming immediately. While we had training in defensive tactics if the situation became confrontational, let's just say I was going to do anything to make sure this would not occur. The driver was a Native American, which could become an issue, since the reservation was considered a sovereign nation, which excluded Native Americans from some state and federal taxes.

Off the reservation, Native Americans had to obey all laws, which sometimes became an issue depending on whether it was the government or Native Americans deciding where the border was.

On this stop, what I did not expect was the biggest human being I'd ever seen step out of the cab. Of course, within a few minutes, the crowd observing went from a few to twenty-five.

I turned to my partner and asked her to call for backup to the state police barracks. I knew Investigator Payne could definitely handle herself, but I wanted backup before the situation became worse, since the onlookers were becoming very vocal. While awaiting backup, I explained to this bear in men's clothing why he'd been pulled over.

He rebutted my explanation, saying that "the white man's law did not apply to him." At that moment, I knew, between the crowd becoming larger and louder and the bear man telling me he did not believe in white man's law, I'd made the right call on backup. The response from the troopers was immediate.

But before I could relax and enjoy the moment, the two troopers exited their vehicle. I'm not saying they were short, but their Stetsons could not be seen over the roof of the state police vehicle. In police work, like in many other jobs, it's not about size, it's about being able to do the job, your experience, and how you handle yourself in dangerous situations.

So, when I asked the troopers how long they'd been on the job, Bambi responded, "We've been out of the academy two months. We were roommates in the academy and now we're partners." My partner looked at me with an expression that said, "What the fuck!"

"Okay," I responded, trying to think about how not to get an ass whooping. How they were not with a training officer shocked me. To be professional, I kept my mouth shut. Also, my past working relationship with troopers had been excellent, and the ones I worked with always had my back.

It was at this time I decided to go into the Billy bullshit with the truck driver. I said, "I respect your thoughts about sovereignty, so here's what we should do. I am about to issue you an appearance ticket, which gives you the opportunity to explain your side in court. An appearance ticket is just what it says, the individual is required to show up in court in response to this summons." This avoided arresting him on scene, which, between the crowd and Mountain Man Dean, let's just say it would not have gone well. Also, I knew my partner's and my handcuffs would never fit Mr. Dean.

I kept my cool throughout the situation until Bambi questioned how I handled things. "Why did you not arrest him and put him in handcuffs?"

I said, "Did you see the crowd and the hostility building?"

"That should not have mattered," she responded.

My only reply was, "Well, when you have a few more years on the job, maybe you'll have a different approach." I thanked them and told them to stay safe, which I knew was possible.

Last I heard, after a couple of incidents, they were both transferred downstate, but to different barracks.

[5]
DEATH

For all the death I've seen, I will never forget standing in front of the downed World Trade Center from the 9/11 attack a couple of days afterward. With only one of the towers and the scene beyond, it looked like a war zone.

I was having trouble breathing and assumed it was from the still-smoldering "pile" of ruins. I did not realize I was experiencing a panic attack. These "attacks" were becoming more frequent.

Later, I realized the first time I had these symptoms was six years earlier, in the summer of 1995.

I was returning to my office in Plattsburgh on a Sunday, having just finished a swim in Schroon Lake. While continuing my drive up Route 87, I observed multiple cars pulled over on both sides of the northbound lanes, and beyond that, I could see people exiting their cars and running down the median from the elevated southbound lane.

Putting my police lights on my unmarked car, I exited the

vehicle, and walked about twenty feet to where people were stopping and trying to help. It took a few seconds to comprehend what I was seeing. Multiple people dressed in what I believed at the time to be Pakistani traditional dress were walking and kneeling in the sloping median, screaming. Some had multiple injuries. While racing back to my vehicle, I saw a middle-aged woman screaming for me to help her husband. As I approached her, I saw a man with his skull crushed and part of his brains on the shoulder of the highway. Even though there was nothing I could do for him, I checked for a pulse. Of course, there was none. My mind was racing, but I knew I had to go back to my vehicle to call for assistance.

The grieving woman held on to my arm. I tried to explain that I needed to call for help. Obviously she was hysterical, and even though I wanted to try and counsel her, I could not. Once back at the vehicle, I called out over my police radio my call sign, 7b90—which identified which police vehicle was transmitting—asking for assistance for a motor vehicle accident with multiple injuries from any road patrol near the location, Rte. 87, mile marker 86, northbound lane.

Immediately, a state police vehicle responded. I repeated the information, trying to maintain proper radio transmission, or at least to this day I hope I did. State police responded, "Be there in 04," meaning four minutes.

I grabbed my beach towel and ran back to the scene to put my towel over the man and try to comfort the hysterical woman.

Thank God one of the uninjured passengers from the vehicle came over and sat with her so I could try to ascertain the injuries of the people in the median. By this time, a nurse and an off-duty EMT were assisting. A sense of relief came over me until they told me their phones were not working, which is common in the mountains between Schooner Lake and Plattsburgh. Best-case scenario, phone coverage works intermittently.

Right then, a passerby came up to us and said there was a passenger from the vehicle almost cut in half on the southbound guard rail. Could someone check on him? The medical professionals said they would. Again, my mind raced, thinking, *How do I say no?* I knew there was nothing I could do, while the nurse and EMT tried to assist whoever they could.

My thoughts returned to where the hell the trooper was, so I ran to my car, thinking it had been twenty minutes, and transmitted over the radio. "We have multiple fatalities. Where are you?" negating all proper radio procedures.

The trooper responded, "I'm pulling up on the scene now."

I've always had respect for troopers, but that day, it grew even more. The trooper was so professional. He advised me he had radioed for medical and police presence and asked me, "Is there medical personnel on scene?"

I responded, "Yes."

He then took care of traffic control, and while he did so, he advised me if I had any police clothing in my vehicle to put it on, seeing as I was still dressed in swim trunks, a T-shirt, and flip-flops. Somewhat embarrassed, I stated, "Thanks, that's a good idea."

When I returned with a police jacket, hat, and badge, the trooper observed my rank on my badge and said, "I arrived in 04."

I became even more embarrassed, but from this accident, I

now have the greatest respect for not only road patrol troopers and all other cops that have road patrol duties. Another lesson learned for "Billy the Liquor Guy."

Finally, when I arrived in Plattsburgh, I went directly to my favorite bar, J.C. Jazz Club—no, it's not a jazz bar, the new owner just kept the name. I was a regular there.

After I ordered my Jack and Coke, Steve, the owner, asked, "You okay? You look white as a ghost."

I said, "No, make it a double."

[PART 2]

MY LIFE

[6]
BOULEVARD OF BROKEN DREAMS

In my neighborhood growing up, you were either a cop or a crook. Suffice to say, a few people were not happy I chose the cop route. After returning to my hometown, I started running into people I'd known over fifty years, primarily at Marr-Logg House, a restaurant in Utica. I had a flashback to Whitey's diner, an old East Utica hangout.

One of the most memorable experiences was one snowy and cold Monday morning. Due to all the customers coming and going, the door seemed to be opening constantly. I can still see Dave and Chris making breakfast and Dick Briggs at the table in the middle of Whitey's breaking everyone's balls as they came in and out. Dicky was a funny bastard who had a knack at picking out each person's special talent or an issue of no talent. I actually played ball with Dicky, but all his brothers were the real athletes in the family. From running to football, his brothers all were sectional champ caliber.

Joe became one of the best referees in my section. Dicky, not so much.

I am a bit prejudiced, because during my son's sectional championship run, Dicky made one of the worst calls I've ever seen. I say this with a bit of experience from playing high school football and coaching.

But my real confirmation and satisfaction came later while running into Dicky and the Briggs brothers at Marr-Logg and sitting with them while they were finishing up breakfast.

Billy the Liquor Guy was doing what he did best and what made him a damn good undercover agent: table hopping, talking to everybody, working the room. But instead of buying guns, drugs, and bombs, I was promoting my book.

After a few pleasantries, Dicky immediately bought a book. I told him, "This does not let you off the bullshit call twenty-two years ago."

Before Dick could respond in his usually quick wit, both his brothers said in unison, "Worst call ever seen."

Brother Joe added he was screaming from the stands, "Bullshit call!"

Seeing Joe was head of the officials and designated the assignments, it did lessen the sting a bit.

If you read my first book or was assigned the excruciating task of transcribing my undercover taped audio, you definitely can testify that I do wander all over with my conversation. One compliment—and I hate to do this to Dicky—is that he did come up with the phrase "Boulevard of Broken Dreams." The county executive was the first to remember the Boulevard as he was a product of that environment and a definite success story.

Okay, back to the title of this chapter, Boulevard of Broken Dreams, and that cold winter day at Whitey's and my somewhat criminal friends.

While I was enjoying eggs, sausage, home fries, and toast, two acquaintances of mine who had criminal records came in but were not their normal ball-breaking selves. They sat way in the back of Whitey's away from everyone else and appeared to be involved in a serious conversation. They left so quietly I must admit I didn't even see them leave. So much for sharp investigation.

It was not long after arriving at my parents' house that I heard and saw numerous police cars speeding up and down the street. Home was only a few blocks from Whitey's, but more importantly, as I would find out later, they were looking for two guys who had robbed a bank, which was also a few blocks from my parents' house.

Before anyone makes any cracks about my work ethic, I was at my parents' having an early lunch. Yes, a few hours had passed since breakfast at Whitey's

I wanted to know what all the activity was about, and I knew the place to find out was Whitey's.

I walked through that damn door that never shut, and even though it was early afternoon, the place was cold. Within the hours that had passed with the heat kicking in, cooking being on, and additional body heat, you'd have thought Whitey's would have warmed up, but it didn't.

Once in, I noticed the lack of heat immediately because I saw those same two acquaintances with criminal records sitting at a table, now with a third person I didn't know. They were in a much more jovial attitude, pointing at each other and laughing. I remember asking Dave and Chris what was going on, and they just said, "Nothing."

I sat down at a table with a long-time friend, Bob Ferdula, and asked him the same question. His response was, "No clue."

It took me a moment to realize this was a typical response when something big had occurred or was about to, so I just drank my coffee and engaged in small talk. Even Dicky Briggs, who was also there for lunch, had no comedic insults toward anybody.

All my questions were answered, as were everyone else's at Whitey's, when a half-dozen Utica police officers and three detectives came through the door, telling everyone to put their hands on top of the tables and to keep quiet.

The officers and detectives approached the tables in pairs. They then proceeded to tell each customer to identify themselves, which I found hilarious, because I knew the police officers already knew everyone, since most were regulars at Whitey's.

The owner was the first to speak up, telling the officers, "We're going to have a grease fire if we do not take care of the stove and grill."

A couple of cops who were regulars told Chris and Dave to continue cooking, much to the displeasure of one of the detectives. Needless to say, that asshole was not from East Utica and had definitely not been to Whitey's before.

Eventually the detectives made their way to the table in the back of the room and started questioning the three individuals seated there. It was obvious this table was their target from the beginning.

After a few responses from these guys along the lines of, "Kiss my ass," and, "If you're arresting me, I want my lawyer," one of the older cops said, "We're going down to the police station to talk about this. Chris, can we use the phone so the gentlemen can call their attorney?"

"Absolutely," Chris said.

Then the officer explained. "They are going to handcuff you guys for your protection and ours," assuring them they would arrive at the police station in the same condition they were in leaving Whitey's. All three men agreed.

Three things I learned that day: take charge, be respectful, and explain what is going to happen in the next few minutes, stating the positive and negative results pending the choices they make.

The other lesson was that if altercations do occur, once the handcuffs are on, the fighting stops.

The driver of the getaway vehicle from the bank robbery was identified by patrons in the parking lot of the East Utica bank. T.B., who went into the bank with J.D., eventually ratted on J.D. for a lighter sentence.

Both the driver and J.D. received twenty years due to priors. T.B. received ten for cooperating.

The Boulevard of Broken Dreams snake bit all three. T.B. was killed right across from Whitey's, just two weeks after getting out of prison, coming out of a social club on the Boulevard. He was shot execution style. Another unsolved murder in the city that used to be called Sin City.

One more thing about the Whitey's and Marr-Logg connection.

On another visit to Marr-Logg, I greeted Joe, one of the

regulars, who happened to be sitting with retired cops, the bank president, and the funeral director. All of them were breaking my balls about the $1.3 million that purportedly got lost under my watch (reference my first book). "We know you took it. You have it buried?"

"My bank is not taking any large cash deposits," said the bank president, suggesting it was dirty.

My response always was, "I have no knowledge of the missing money, and I did not take any $1.3 million."

Joe put his coffee down, looked straight at me, and said, "So how much did you take?"

Best line ever. There's an old East Utica guy for ya.

[7]
BAD YEAR

On December 13, 1995, while returning from a law enforcement conference in Ottawa, Canada, my boss—and good friend—and I were hit by a really bad snowstorm when we reached Watertown, NY. The snow-covered roads continued to make for a tense trip. Near Boonville, Route 12 was blocked due to a motor vehicle accident. We were directed to take a detour on some back roads to avoid the accident. This was actually a break from the tense driving because we had the opportunity to follow a snowplow, which not only plowed the road in front of us, but the lights from the snow plow illuminated the road immensely, which made it a hell of a lot better than the tension-filled ride we had been experiencing for the last few hours.

Once we returned to Route 12, the plow left us to plow the road that had been shut down.

I remember telling George, "Well, we're almost home."

I told him that for two reasons—one to try to give him

more support and hopefully relax him a bit from this stressful driving, and second to perk me up and realize we had less than twenty minutes to go before home.

While approaching the last hill (Deerfield Hill) before Mohawk Valley, with swirling snow limiting visibility to a few feet, in a short break in the blinding snow, I thought for a second that I saw something crossing the four-lane highway, but it disappeared. I was just saying to George, "Did you—" when something hit our car and then came into our windshield. Then it fell off to the side.

At that instant, George and I looked at each other and said, "What the Christ was that?" Then, right after that, we heard these bone-chilling screams.

George said, "We hit someone." While George put our reds on and called for assistance, I exited the car and saw a person lying on the road.

The screaming subsided a little. All I heard in between the moans was, "Help me."

I responded, "We've got you. An ambulance is on the way." I tried to comfort her as much as I could. I kept telling her help was on the way and asking if she was cold, even though I could not hear her. I took off my winter coat and put it on her. I held her hand and kept repeating, "Help is coming."

At this time, I was wondering where George was. I started hollering his name. Suddenly, he came up the slope from the median and said, "There's a guy in a car that went off the road. He's okay, just scared."

Finally, we started to hear sirens and make out flashing lights coming over the hill. We both kept telling her, "Help is here." The ambulance arrived but passed us on Rte. 12 northbound.

When it went past, I yelled, "Where the hell is he going?"

George said, "Billy, he is looking for a way to get across."

It seemed like eternity before the ambulance arrived. The EMTs rushed over and took control of the situation.

Right after that, I saw a police vehicle coming down the southbound lane. All I could think about was that this was the second time within a few months that I was relieved to see those flashing lights.

When the state police arrived, a captain introduced himself.

I thought, *Why the hell is a captain responding to a motor vehicle accident?* Then he asked to see our police credentials, and it hit me. Whether it was the cold air or the fact that once I got to thinking after all that'd happened in how I felt for this lady and her injuries and the relief that help had arrived, we were personally involved in a serious motor vehicle accident.

When the captain advised we should get out of the cold but assigned us to separate vehicles, my mind flashed back to my younger years when I was directed to the back of a police car to be questioned. Due to George's rank, the captain interviewed George, and I was interviewed by the zone sergeant.

Of course, the first question he asked was if I was okay. "Yes," I answered.

"Where are you coming from?"

"Ottawa, for a police conference."

"Who was driving?"

I answered, "George."

"Were you drinking?"

I answered, "No." Then I thought, *Thank God, because of the bad weather, we left immediately and did not stay for happy hour.*

The sergeant then took me to the captain's car where George was being interviewed. While walking to the car, I noticed the ambulance was still on scene. I said, "Fuck," and a cold shiver went through my body, but not due to the freezing weather.

The next thing George said to me was that the ambulance had not moved. My shoulders slumped, and I bowed my head, thinking I was going to vomit. George asked the question to the captain, even though we both knew the answer. "Yes, she has died, gentlemen. I am sorry." It was 5:26 p.m. I will never forget that.

We then were transported to the nearest trooper barracks, which oddly was only two miles from my house, although at this time, it seemed a thousand miles away. At the barracks, where I'd conducted many interrogations myself, we were questioned intensely.

After an accident reconstruction, they concluded that the weather was the major contributing factor. Also, the fact that the idiot—my thoughts—who had gone off the road partly due to the conditions was driving with his poodle on his lap.

"Fucking moron," I said out loud inside the troopers' barracks once I stopped ranting at the trooper's questions.

They then explained that the lady had exited her vehicle to assist this idiot—again, my words—and she didn't realize she was in the middle of the passing lane when she was talking to him.

I had forgotten we went around another car because it

was driving erratically, and we stayed in the passing lane because there were deeper tracks that made the driving easier.

Before we left, the captain suggested that, even though it was obvious we were not drinking, we should get a blood test to have documentation.

This was also suggested by George's brother, who came to bring us home.

So up to the hospital we went to get our bloodwork. When I finally got home, I went inside, put boots on, and walked around my neighborhood yelling and cursing with tears running down my cheeks. I was out so long that my face had icicles on it.

I was too wound up to sleep. Eventually, I just changed from my suit into my casual work clothes and went to work. Dave was waiting for me to arrive. He played a soft role at first but quickly warmed up to his typical demeanor.

"You're not going to be a fucking pussy about this and crack up on me, are you?" he joked.

"Fuck you," I responded. I wanted to be upset with his cold statement, but hearing his usual talk put me at ease and gave me an odd sense that, eventually, everything would be back to how it had been. For now, I just needed to find a way to get through the eventually part.

"You're required to see Father Joe before you enter the field," Mills told me after pulling me into his office to hear how I was. "He specializes in helping officers involved in fatalities."

My body filled with dread. The last person I wanted to see was Father Joe. He was a priest designed to help officers who had some real mental shit going on so they could go back in the field.

"I'm not fucked up," I said to Mills. "I just need to work. What happened was a choice they took from God's hands."

"What's done is done, but you ignoring the help you need to get you through this in a healthy manner. If you do that, you will keep what happened with you forever," Mills replied. "You can choose to be an asshole and refuse to see Father Joe, or you can take a step in the right direction and handle your shit so you can get back to work."

I chose the latter. I went to see Father Joe the next morning. To my surprise, it wasn't a total loss. There wasn't a lot of Bible talk or repentance like in my younger days at church. Instead, Father Joe gave me some inspiring advice that I continue to turn to years later.

"God chooses people to take on a horrific event because he knows they're strong enough to handle it," he said. "Therefore, he put you in that place at the time." If I am fortunate to get into Heaven, I definitely will bring this up with Jesus Christ and tell him that, due to all the nightmares I have when I do sleep, he made the wrong call on this.

"Sometimes people also give up the right to live," he told me. "When someone pulls a gun on a cop or speeds through a lighted railroad crossing, they give up their right to live. As hard as it may be to accept that this lady who chose to get out of her car also gave up the right to live, she decided to make her own choice."

I mulled over his words, thinking of George and the exact timing with our leaving early, our bathroom stop, etc. Over the years, I would find myself at various times dissecting those words and reevaluating how they worked.

George and I went back to work as usual, never speaking of the accident or the woman we killed. It wouldn't be until the summer that we would approach the matter again.

Per Father Joe's words, I think it was a perfect storm that put us there. The storm itself, us leaving early, the bathroom break we took at McDonald's, and both bathrooms that were occupied, the detour, the wrecked driver we passed, and staying in the passing lane for better traction. Well, it's been twenty-six years since the accident, and I hope I am fortunate to have another twenty-plus years on God's green earth, but when I do see Jesus Christ, I am still going to mention it.

[8]

BAD YEAR CONTINUED

The next bad news happened after George and I went to a police conference at Kennebunkport, ME in July. The conference itself was great. I was thrilled to get away. Work had been hectic; our caseload had doubled with the Native American smuggling, and we had a full crew of state police, local police, ICE, PATB units, and border patrol all wrapped into one.

As an avid swimmer, I couldn't wait to dive into the coast. I spent the six-hour drive to Maine salivating over the waves and salty water that awaited us. But in July, that water was still cold as hell.

George tried the water first, and leaped like a spring out of the ocean, hollering from the shock of the icy cold waters. Of course, that just made me want to dive in even more. At least, that's how I saw it.

We were so eager to get into the water that I ignored the private property signs all around us that said the beach was closed. Our conference location was Suttner, the location of George Bush's private estate, and it turned out that the beach we were at was actually part of his property. My friend George was laughing because my scream from jumping into the cold water had attracted the attention of Bush's Secret Service, who were currently running down the beach toward me. By the time they scooped me from the water, my broad, hairy chest shivering under the warm sun, George was in full hysterics. He couldn't wait to tell everyone at the conference what I had done.

When George and I went to check into the hotel, I was still a bit wet. A woman checking in asked us, "Oh, is there a pool here?" George simply replied, "No," to her. Then he pointed to me and said, "Oh, him? He's an idiot."

The rest of the weekend went great, but a steady stream of food, room service, and some interesting investigators ready to stay at the bar all night meant George couldn't get comfortable. His back had been bothering him from the drive. Though he claimed it was just a kink he couldn't work out, I knew it was something more when he asked me to leave the retreat early on Sunday morning. I drove the whole way home while George slept.

The following morning, George called in sick and, thanks to a push from his wife, went to see his doctor. It would be George's wife who called me later that afternoon to let me know that George was in the hospital. He'd been diagnosed with a rare type of blood cancer.

When I saw him in the hospital that same evening, George looked hollow and pale, and was blanketed by oxygen masks, tubes, and wires, providing him with fresh, healthy blood.

He'd been asleep for some time, but the nurse assured me he would be waking up shortly for his next dose of medication.

Since George always had a good sense of humor, I headed to the hallway, grabbed a vacant gurney, and wheeled it into the room beside George. The nurse, who was about to scold me, stepped back and listened to my pleading case of friendship in humor.

Reluctantly, she watched as I placed myself up on the gurney, wrapped in a white sheet, and moved the blood between us. When George came to, he sat up, and in confusion looked at the pole, the blood, then the nurse, who was cautiously waiting for his reaction. "Please say they did not give me your blood," he pleaded. "I don't know if I can live knowing your blood is inside me."

I sat up, throwing back the sheets and exposing my clean arm. The joke sparked a smile from George, me, and even the nurse, and led to an evening with George filled with funny stories and jokes about cases prior.

"Billy," George said, his body slowly sinking back in the comfort of his bed. "You think I have cancer because I killed that lady?"

The comment caught me off guard.

"I killed her, Billy," he said for the first time. "I hit that lady and killed her. I think this is my punishment."

"Will you be fucking serious?" I said, leaning forward to look at him. "If people were given illnesses every time they made a mistake or did something wrong in life, the world would be dead."

George looked down, his eyes filled with tears yet to fall.

"Look at me, for crying out loud," I continued. "If that's

how you think, then I should have leprosy for all the shit I've done in my life."

"You are a crooked son of a bitch." George laughed.

"Exactly," I added. "And ain't shit happened to me yet. So you should be in the clear."

"Let's hope that's the truth." George smiled, the tears finally exiting his eyes and rolling down his cheeks.

"If you really want a fighting chance, though, you should take my blood," I teased, easing back into my chair.

"Not on your life."

George spent some time in the hospital recuperating. The doctor said they found the cancer early enough, so they were able to fight it off with some transfusions and chemo. The doctor told George he was lucky to have caught the cancer when he did. But they left him with an understanding: Should the cancer return, the outlook may not be as good.

George put up a fight. He hit it strong and gave it everything he had. He remained on the force, working long hours to keep his mind from what was going on inside his body. But no matter how hard he fought, the cancer fought harder. George died at the end of March.

His funeral was held on April 1st, which did add some levity for Jimmy Simpson, who delivered the eulogy. It seemed like George had his final hurrah. However, as much as I found humor in the date and the stories that filled the service, I couldn't avoid the hatred and spite I felt upon spotting Booth there. He'd arrived in the middle of the service, wearing a white T-shirt, blue jeans, and a black motorcycle jacket.

The funeral was a full police funeral. Everyone was dressed in uniforms, with bagpipes playing in the background and a police barricade to escort George to the cemetery. Booth, however, despite his customary suit and tie, opted at this one time to remain casual. He also made sure to exit the service before the family even had a chance to rise from their seats.

As I drove home from the funeral, my mind was clouded with visions of George and Booth. I couldn't let go of the hatred I felt for Booth being there, and just in casual clothes. He had no right to sit in a pew pretending to grieve over George. All Booth ever did was bitch that George should never have been promoted over him. First of all, Booth was an ass-kisser and only kept his job because of the politics; he'd never passed the civil service test, and even though he'd been with the agency a long time, he'd never had a major arrest.

Probably the reason I am so focused on Booth is because I'm writing this on the twenty-year anniversary of 9/11, and like everyone else, I remember where I was. Booth was not a chief yet, but he was my superior, and I was in his office in Albany inquiring why he was always breaking my balls.

The day before, Monday, September 10th, Booth had requested my arrival at the scene of another officer's arrest. I denied his request based on my current involvement in another takedown and lack of a partner. Booth attempted to call my bluff, contacting Mills and filing an official ordinance against me.

When I received notification from Mills, I was enraged.

"I don't know what you did to rub this guy the wrong way," Mills said, showing me a piece of paper. "But you've got to find a way to end it. He's written you up on disobedience charges, says you're not following through with his calls and are becoming incompliant."

I pulled the paper from Mills' hands and threw it in the trash. "I'm not signing that shit, and I'm not answering his calls."

"Billy," Mills said, sighing, "this is getting exhausting. You are both grown men. You're going to have to find a commonality."

"That you'd have to pay me extra for." I smiled at Mills.

Mills ran his fingers through his hair and looked right at me with his piercing blue eyes.

"I have proof and times of where you were, so let's not worry about it," Mills said. "Keep your head up and don't respond directly to Booth. Are we clear?"

Then Mills added, "You know, you're one giant pain in the ass. You're one hell of an investigator, but man, you're one hell of a pain."

"Yeah, well, I like you, too, Mills," I joked.

At this time, Mills had me busy at work, and Dave had quit, leaving me partnerless. So I was rendered to working the field alone, now struggling with the absence of two of my closest allies.

As for me? If you know anything about me, you know I wasn't going to take Mills' advice when it came to Booth. It was as clear as Tuesday morning when I woke up the next day, hours before my shift, and flew down to Booth's office, ready to confront him once and for all.

As I barged past the doors, I could hear Booth's secretary calling his phone. "Booth, Bill is on his way into your office."

Booth barely had time to hang up the phone before I was standing over him, ready for a fight. The years of aggravation, the accident, Dave's departure, George's death, and a write-up had all come to a hard boil.

"You think you're so fucking smart," I said, looking down at Booth, still seated in his chair. "You ain't shit. All you are is a selfish motherfucker who's scared shitless of a job he can't handle. A job he's not equipped for."

Booth tried to rise from his seat, but I pushed my body closer, forcing him back down. "You wouldn't even be sitting where you are now if it wasn't for me," I spat. "Your dumb ass couldn't even pass a test for this position. Is that what you're so scared of? Are you scared that people will find out that the one investigator you can't stand is the one who gave you this job? I wonder what people would say if they found out." I pulled the test scores from my back pocket and waved them over his head.

"That's all you've got?" Booth laughed. "You're so proud to hang that over my head. How long are you gonna hold onto that, huh? How long until you accept that I'm your boss? I tell you what you can and can't do, and that is what really bothers you."

Booth forced his way up from his seat, leaving less than an inch of space between us. "You think you're going to come into my office now and speak to me like this, just because you have some paper," he said between gritted teeth. "I'd love to see what your next plan of action is, besides this illegal spin of blackmail you're trying out."

"You stupid bastard." I leaned in, our noses so close they were almost touching. "You're so keen on breaking my balls." I shoved my chest into Booth, causing him to take a step backward. "Let's see what you actually have, you gutless fuck."

Booth lunged at me, grabbing me by my shirt collar. I shoved him again, this time with my hands, and he went flying back into his chair.

He stood up, his eyes bulging, and charged at me. I was ready for it. I could almost taste the sweet victory of my fist landing hard across his face, but two officers came barreling into the room, separating us.

"Let me go, Hogan," Booth sneered, trying to pull away from his officer's hold. "This isn't your job. Let me go."

"Yeah, let him go so he can finally take his soft punch," I spat. "He's good at letting others do the real work."

More officers came into the room, trying to break up the ruckus, both struggling to come at me. "You stupid assholes!" an officer suddenly yelled, taking both Booth and me by surprise. "The Towers have been hit. Do you hear me? A plane has just flown into the Twin Towers in New York City."

Booth and I were foaming at the mouth, our bodies tightly held back by other officers. "The governor is demanding all people to their posts at once!" the officer yelled to Booth. "All offices are on high alert. They think this is a possible act of terrorism."

Booth flung off his officer and scrambled to the phone, while I stood up, straightened out my shirt, now stretched out at the neck, and checked my phone. No call from Mills. I walked out of the office, passed the team of officers staring at me, and into the lobby to call my office.

"Billy," Bobby answered, "have you heard? The Towers

were hit. They're asking us to close the office so we can secure all federal stations and buildings."

"Did they direct everyone where to go?"

"Yes, you're going to the State Building. They want all points covered."

"Got it."

"Billy," Bobby's voice cracked, "stay in contact and be safe."

"Same to you," I responded. "Let everyone know where I'll be."

I jumped in my car and headed down to Albany, dialing our NYC office in the Twin Towers again and again. Mills was supposed to be there today. The phone didn't connect. I tried Mills again. Nothing.

By the time I arrived at the state office building, it was flooded with officers. I checked in at the post and was sent to guard the main building, along with five other officers. I wasn't at the front gate for more than two minutes before the first tower went down. I could hear the screams and cries over the radio dispatch. I stood still, my eyes frantically looking in each direction. For the first time in my career, I was lost and needed someone to tell me what was happening and what to do, but there was no one to turn to. The other officers were just as confused and scared as I was.

Then the second tower went down.

All the radio waves were silent. Then, just as quickly as the air broke, shouts and hysteria filled the radio once again. The sound of officers yelling, floor numbers being shouted, and names being broadcast over the line left me standing there feeling hopeless.

For the next few hours, we stood guard, all wondering about our fellow teammates. By two o'clock, I was told the chance of survivors from our office, which was located in the South Tower, was very grim. This news nearly suffocated me. Names and faces ran through my mind faster than I could catch my breath.

"You okay?" the officer to my right asked, placing his hand on my shoulder. "You need to sit down." Out of the blue, a familiar voice filled the ringing that was vibrating through my ears.

"That pussy excuse for an investigator doesn't need shit," Booth said, approaching me. "Don't play into his whiny routine."

Booth stopped directly in front of me. "Who's got your back now, asshole?" He smiled. I was so shocked by his words that I just stood there, my mouth hanging open, unable to say a word. My brain couldn't process anything that was happening. Booth smiled even larger, gave a slight laugh at my lack of response, and walked away.

I was certain I heard him whistling as he gleefully went to back up his crew. Even though I realized Booth was a piece of shit, my mind continued to spin, to think this asshole was happy about Mills' death was inconceivable.

We received confirmation of Mills' death in less than twenty-four hours. When the planes hit, Mills immediately dismissed his officers and assisted in leading people to the exits. Mills, who was always a stand-up guy, didn't ignore the cries for help. He stopped to help those who had fallen, those who were being trampled, and those who were frozen in fear. For weeks, people would come forward and tell the tale of the man inside the stairwell who saved their lives. And at his funeral, Mills' wife stood at the podium and described how her husband had saved so many lives who would have become trapped, and perished with the building. That was his character. She said, "He died, remaining true to who he was and doing what was instilled in him. He died as a hero."

I kept these words, and the stories of the people he saved, with me as I tried to imagine how I was to go on from here.

[PART 3]
BACK TO WORK

[9]
THREE-FOR-ONE IN A DAY

Early on the cig ops, when we were working on cigarette cases out of New York City, Stanton called and told us we had to shut down for a few days until we were able to obtain money for larger amounts of cig product.

Of everyone I met, the person who would leave the biggest impact on me by far was Tom Stanton. As readers of *Under Too Long* know, Stanton was responsible for the success I had during my undercover career. He was the one who gave me the freedom I needed to be who I needed to be and allowed me to create outside of the box. Because of his mentality and leadership, I was able to stay in my role as Billy the Liquor Guy and push past my abilities.

After Stanton come Tony, El Bobbo, Jeff Who, and Redneck Randy—all tied for second. Besides being a great undercover agent, Tony was the perfect partner. He dealt with all of my crazy shit during my initial undercover work. El

Bobbo and Jeff were like brothers—who happened to go through some dangerous times with me. As I'm sure most people understand, when dangerous or crazy things happen, people like your brothers are who you want by your side. Now, Redneck Randy, well, let's just say he accepted me for who I was—most of the time. But I digress.

Anyway, the state was concerned about "going into the cigarette business" due to the fact the ops were becoming larger and larger where we needed hundreds of cases of cigarettes.

Mind you, Tom had presented the plan months before. He'd advised the powers that be of utilizing area informants' storage facilities and audio and video equipment. Basically, it was a carbon copy of his successful sting operations from when he was heading the New York City Tax Agency.

In defense of the suits, the ops did grow really quickly, and they wanted to reevaluate the amount of money needed.

Additionally, even though the ops were paying for themselves, the agents worked overtime and had hotel stays, storage activities, and car rentals. Add to that the New York State's Attorney's concerns about entrapment during the sales of cigarettes to customers.

I guess the undercovers should've noticed the danger, seeing we were entering the world of organized crime and terrorist groups. But, speaking for the undercovers and the team I was working with, we did not give a shit. We all were hooked, especially now considering the dirtbags responsible for 9/11 and the deaths of our coworkers and thousands of innocent people killed at the Towers, the Pentagon, and in Shanksville, PA.

Back to the entrapment issue, the government agents may not originate a criminal design or implant an idea in an innocent person's mind. The disposition to commit a criminal act must be there so that the government may prosecute.

In simple English, undercovers may not offer, for example, a case of cigarettes for $1000 when the average price is around $2,500, depending on the brand. In that case, the deal is so great, you are enticing them to purchase it.

As Billy the Liquor Guy, by this time, I had made hundreds of sales, and not only had been advised by New York State Attorneys about entrapment, but from twenty-plus years of being a street investigator and having common sense, I was quite versed in it, as were the other undercovers.

Okay, I'm getting to the three-for-one day and Captain Coupon.

If you have read my first book or listened to any of my interviews and podcasts, you know I am never at a shortage for veering off the issue, which was very beneficial in years of undercover work.

Also if you have read the first book or caught Tom Stanton on Disruption Network, EC Radio, hosted by the Zee, you will know Tom is not the waiting type. Tom reached out to Randy to see if he had any of the same ops in the works. Randy advised Tom an informant had told him a sandwich truck company in Queens was selling untaxed cigarettes out of its truck. Per computer records, this company had over sixty trucks selling out of the New York City area. Tom said to check it out, and if they made contact to bring me along.

Randy was the smartest street investigator I'd ever met and

also a computer whiz at research, which more than a few of us street cops were not.

Randy met with me and said he had called the owner and set up a meeting for the afternoon to discuss purchasing a few sandwich trucks for upstate New York and to make sure the owner would know we would not infringe on his area.

Randy said he would play the part of the businessman during our meeting,. He had already researched information about the sandwich truck operations and the cost of trucks, both new and used. He would say he was there to purchase some used trucks because he was just starting out. My job was to mention the fact that I owned a bar years ago and had contacts to pick cheaper food products—yes, even beer and liquor. Did I mention Randy had a bigger set of balls than me and would throw it right out there that he had to make money as quickly as possible? And I would claim that I had no problem evading some stupid laws that made it impossible for a businessman to make any real money.

I was all prepared, and Randy reminded me again to go into one of my bullshit stories if the opportunity arose.

I was thinking, *No pressure, right?*

Did I mention Randy says it like it is and wanted no part of lazy workers because he expected his team members to work as long as it took to get the job done, which I could attest to because of all the twenty-hour days we worked.

Also, he had a saying: If you have to get your wife's okay for the overtime, get the combination to your safe from your wife, go and get your balls out, and put them back in your pants. But don't even think about joining the team.

Randy was just that no-nonsense type of guy.

So there Randy and I were, walking into this business in Queens. First thing I noticed was all these trays of hot dogs in uncovered pans just sitting out on wood pallets, which were all over the garage floor. We had to walk around them to get to this owner's office. Needless to say, I will never eat another hot dog unless I cook it myself. The owner was Russian and spoke very broken English. Randy told the owner, Egor, what he was looking for and that if the price was right he could purchase a half-dozen used trucks. He added that if we bought the trucks, he would handle the financing, and payment would be all in cash.

There was my opening. Enter Billy the Liquor Guy. After a couple shots of vodka with Egor, the conversation flowed a little easier.

I added that, for my bar business to make some extra cash, I'd buy untaxed or stolen liquor.

You could see the guy was interested by his eyes opening wider and his leaning toward me.

"So how do you get liquor?" he asked.

I came right back with, "Like I do with all my product. I buy in the states with little taxes. New Hampshire for liquor. For cigs, I buy in Virginia."

Bam, right to the point, and like Randy said, get it done. I also told Egor I was working through a contact to purchase cigs off the Poospatuck Reservation, which was in the community of Mastic in Suffolk County.

It was one of the first times where some shit was in the back of my mind and it just came out. This information had come from Tom a few days earlier. Some New York City guys had arrested a guy in a rental Ryder truck who was making deliveries in New York City from cigs coming off the Poospatuck Reservation.

Tom, being Tom, had detained this guy, Omar, for only an hour and explained he could be released and be on his way to continue with his deliveries that day if he became a paid informant.

The only question Omar asked was, "How do I explain being late for my delivery?" No problem. Within minutes, Tom reached out to a local tow truck company to supply Omar with a receipt for a new tire.

In a little over an hour, Tom had turned Omar, had a new tire put on his truck, and had a receipt in his hand.

Way to go, Tom! A possible in to the Poospatuck Reservation.

Which would be #2 for the day.

Back to Egor. Once he heard about our cigarette prices through Virginia, he wanted in. A new deal was set up for delivery the next day at his garage in Queens. After Egor became comfortable with his new supply of cigs, negating any stealing of his cigs by his lowlife employees (his words), we made deliveries to his multimillion-dollar home in Suffix.

When Egor was taken down by the teams at his garage and home and had all his properties seized a short time later, New York State was extremely happy with the arrest; Egor, not so much

I'm guessing by the reaction of Egor's wife when she too was arrested and their home seized due to storage of stolen property and illegal cigs, she definitely had the key to the safe where his balls would be forever.

To make things look legit, we also had to be arrested on

the final delivery. Even more than the overtime pay, it was worth it to see Egor being ripped apart by his wife firsthand.

This time we were brought in handcuffs to the Suffolk County Jail, which was by far the nicest jail I'd spent any time in.

Throw in the fact that I was paraded through the jail in handcuffs and received a lot of weird looks from other deputies I had worked with prior to the arrest. The sheriff had, as usual, been advised of our participation as undercovers.

The second operation was the Poospatuck Reservation. Tom being Tom, he liked to have multiple ops going, and his brain was always three steps ahead of the bad guys and the suits.

While Tom was turning Omar, he remembered that Omar had said the Poospatucks were running low on cigarettes. They only had about four hundred tribe members living on the reservation. Needless to say, they were the smallest reservation in New York State. When we told Tom we were in the area, he said he'd have some agents run out a few cases to us.

The story I was going to use was that I was near the reservation delivering to some customers and had heard about them from one of them—who I didn't know, due to the fact I was new in the area.

I tried to explain to Tom that with three in a car, we would draw attention. Tom wasn't worried and said that was the way we'd do it. So having far more balls than brains, I proceeded onto the reservation, utilizing Randy and two agents who brought the van and cigs. What could go wrong? Three men sitting in one vehicle near a reservation? We had to be either cops or criminals, and our presence brought attention from both the Native Americans checking out the vehicle and cops getting a call that a suspicious vehicle was parked in the vicinity of the reservation, which was known for criminal activity.

But the thing that made me the most uncomfortable was Tom said I could be one of the few white males to ever be received on the reservation. What the fuck could go wrong?

I told myself fear was good. It kept you on your toes. But I was feeling old and fat, waiting for Billy the Liquor Guy to kick in. I gave my sales pitch that I did not want to offend any sovereign nation, playing ignorant to the fact that this tribe was not recognized as a sovereign nation.

The owner of the store said he wished he could buy a case, saying he had not received his usual delivery, but if he did buy from me, his store would be burned down. The Native Americans did not trust or even like the white man and were very territorial.

As I went to leave, I was confronted by two armed men. I put a smile on this city boy's face, trying to look anything but threatening.

I was checked for weapons. After a few minutes, I was approached by the darkest Native American I'd ever seen. I heard the Poospatucks had a very dark skin color, as did the Shineecock Indian Nation. They were considered black.

This toned, muscular male asked me what the fuck I wanted. Again, I went through my spiel about respecting their sovereignty, then went into my bullshit line about buying cigarettes as I had done before on the Akwesasne Reservation, which covered land in Canada and America near Massena, New York. I threw in even more shit, saying I had smuggled cigarettes through the back roads that exited the reservation that would get you to Malone, Burke, and Chateaugay, New York, which would lead to numerous roads throughout the state. Anyway, my knowledge must've impressed Jim, which was what he said his name was.

Jim invited me into his office where he told me of his hatred of the U.S. government for denying his tribe the sovereign eligibility they deserved. I listened to this bullshit for over an hour before I was finally able to interject that I had to get back on the road. That was when I threw out how many cases of cigarettes I could buy when I was back in the area.

"You got a few more minutes? I want to show you something," Jim said. He took me through a door that led to a small warehouse that had conveyor belts attached to a machine that would sort and cut cigarettes to fit into packs then cartons. I knew this from having had a crash course on how cigarettes were packed. Obviously I played dumb and pretended I was impressed by this secondhand processing machine. I showed interest in the machine, which I knew was not up and running. This was where it paid to throw the bullshit out there to try to get lucky.

Jim asked me if, until the cigarette machine became operable, I would consider buying one hundred cases of cigs at the reservation on the Canadian border.

I was trying to hide my enthusiasm, but I was able to say, "Damn, Jim, I have no idea what size truck I would have to rent to transport that many cases."

Jim said, "A twenty-six footer, and you don't need a class-one license to drive it." He even told me what rental truck company had the best deal.

Okay, now I was buying and transporting cigarettes from a sovereign nation to one that was not. As excited as I was, I thought the possibility of this being forwarded to and being approved by New York State was minimal.

My concerns came to be true. This state was not going to mess with a sovereign nation. It also had an operating casino on the Akwesasne Reservation. The fact this reservation was not paying taxes for cigarette sales—even though the sale of untaxed cigarettes was okay, but only on the reservation to residents and Native Americans—was overlooked due to a pending land claim issue, per a treaty over two hundred years old.

Also the casino was employing hundreds of non–Native Americans, as other casinos did throughout the state, and the state was receiving a tax revenue from these employees. What we were eventually able to do was take down a major illegal cigarette distribution operation. This made the state happy, Indian Affairs happy, had the PATB making points, and made Jim even more pissed.

Op number three was a bit of a stretch but did result in a few arrests in Virginia. Randy asked me to work with him on an upcoming operation that dealt with—in his words—rednecks, which was a fun op nicknamed Redneck Randy (see below for more details on that one!)…. Until I brought a little too much attention to myself and crossed a few too many lines. After the op, I headed back to my hotel to get some much-needed rest. I finally fell asleep about four a.m., thinking, *Damn, I am good!*

I was woken up at about eight a.m. by Randy screaming at me through the phone. "I knew you would cause me grief, you asshole! You're like a hovering black cloud. I don't know who I am more pissed off at: me for not listening to people to stay away from you and not get involved with such an asshole, or you for causing me grief."

Finally, I got a word in even though I had not woken up yet. "Fucking calm down. Let's meet for coffee, which I need desperately. I'll meet you in the lobby."

Downstairs, this five-star Marriott was full of people having breakfast in the restaurant area, so I said, "Let's get our coffees and go for a ride 'cause I am guessing this talk can get ugly."

As soon as we got in the car, Randy's ranting picked up. "You're an asshole. You know how many people don't like you?"

I let him go on and on. When he finally took a breath, I said to Randy something he probably didn't want to hear: "I don't give two fucks who does not like me. Most of the assholes are jealous, and the ones appointed politically are useless."

Randy started up again. "See? That's the reason you were labeled unsupervisable. You don't listen to anybody."

"Randy, how did I do yesterday?" No response. "Randy, why does Plattsburg lead the agency in arrests with half the staff than other offices?" He rolled his eyes. "Why do you think Tom picked me to work undercover?" Before he could answer, I added, "I am not a supervisor type. And I'm not a team player when I am working with idiots and backstabbing motherfuckers. What I am good at is getting the job done."

"Some of that stuff is true," Randy said.

I continued, "What you don't understand is some of these

assholes are just political appointments and those assholes got appointed because they have political capital. Remember those guys from the Syracuse office who did an inspection in the Binghamton area and conducted themselves in a very professional manner, even when the owner jumped over the bar to get their names off their IDs?"

Randy: "Well, smartass, do you know why they were suspended for a month without pay? The bar owner's brother was a state senator. You know that newly appointed supervisor in Buffalo who screamed at me for twenty minutes this morning? How did you think he got appointed? Well, asshole, you remember that boss in New York City that you used to call Yoda because of how short he was?"

Did I remember? Of course I remembered. At a conference, I put a car seat on his chair to tease him about his height.

Randy continued his rant: "That conference we had in Saratoga, you put a kid's car seat on his chair. Even then, you kept breaking his balls when he started screaming shit like, 'I'll have your job, you fuck.' And you kept breaking his balls saying, 'Stand up, I can't hear you,' over and over knowing full well that he was standing up."

Oh, Yoda. The guy who didn't like to come down to the Plattsburg office. The guy with a ton of political contacts. One of the guys I might have pushed too far in my Billy the Liquor Guy mode.

Randy: "Then you went to Shep, who was still the PATB at that time, and said, 'You have my back on this?!' His reply was, 'No fucking way.' If I remember correctly, he continued with, 'You're on your own on this. No one fucks with Manny (Yoda). He's been with the agency for thirty years. He has all the contacts, even wrote some of our manuals, and what Manny wants, Manny gets.'"

I have to admit it was quiet for a while before I came back with, "He's an auditor with a weapon."

Randy: "Again, stupid, Manny likes that shit. He always says auditors bring in millions. They complete an audit and bring in millions in a weekend. Guess what Manny started as… yep, an auditor! But he carries a weapon. Manny gets what Manny wants!"

Randy continued: "If Manny had his way, Upstate would have no offices. When the Plattsburgh office was opened, he was furious. The only reason it was opened was because Ron Stafford was the senior state senator and was chairman of the Senate Finance Committee, and the governors had come to him with their hats in hands to get funding approved. And, genius, remind me who was in charge of that office?"

"Me?" I squeaked.

Randy: "Yep, the moron sitting next to me. That's why Manny did not like you. The Plattsburgh office took funds away from the New York City one. One last thing: How long after Ron Staffer died was the Plattsburgh office closed?"

For the first time ever I did not have a comeback.

After Randy's little fit, I contemplated whether or not to call Captain Coupon (aka Manny) to rip him a new asshole.

I titled him "Captain Coupon" because his one big case was pressing the minimum price issue, which dealt with cigarette coupons. He was one of the few supervisors who was not nice to me.

Of course I decided to give him a call.

As soon as he picked up, I jumped right into the fact that he was not my boss and told him about the ops I'd worked on —the Russian mob, the Poospatuck Native Americans—and the danger involved. Yes, I was referring to his bullshit coupon case that was auditor work. Of course, he came back with the same old shit about me not following orders, and referred to Tom's orders to stand down.

That was when I cut him off. "Well, obviously, you're not in the loop as much as you think, Mr. Asshole, and you know the director of the PATB requested me specifically to go out and work on these cases. So go fuck yourself."

Tom called me later and told me I should not have told the supervisor to fuck off. "Technically, he is in your chain of command. So keep a low profile for a while till I can smooth things over with Manny, understand?"

"Yes, sir!"

[10]
REDNECK RANDY

Redneck Randy, a senior investigator, was the coordinator of all of the operations. He did everything from deciding on the target area to handling confidential informants to be utilized to adding additional team members when needed.

Randy was a workaholic. He loved working even more than "Billy the Liquor Guy." He'd spend critical time reviewing the "operational plan," which included our operation's locality, additional agencies utilized, the positioning of all team members, the profiles of targets, maps of the area, and radio call signs. His reports went further, including local hospitals and each agent's blood type, medical history, and family contact numbers in case an agent should be injured during an operation.

Physically, Randy was a tough bastard who demanded the best of all his team members during our fifteen- to twenty-hour days. When off duty, he was one of our biggest ball breakers. But the thing I enjoyed the most about Randy was the freedom he granted me to be "Billy the Liquor Guy."

Redneck Randy earned his name during the final part of the "three-for-one" operations. While working with me on the sandwich truck case at the Poospatuck Reservation, Randy was in charge of contacting potential customers for cigarette sales in rural Virginia. Through these contacts, his prior cigarette sales informants told him about some good old boys. These guys happened to be on Randy's radar as he'd seen them a couple of weeks back while gassing up his rusty old pickup truck—a very appropriate undercover vehicle he used while driving around Dahlgreen, Virginia.

As the coordinator of all operations, one of Randy's many duties while performing counter-surveillance was looking out for vehicles that could be surveilling ours. When Randy first ran into these guys, he noted their hats, which actually read "Good Old Boys," and their $60,000 truck, which included dusk wheels and an extended back-covered carriage, which was ideal for smuggling. Randy approached them and let out a "Howdy, partner," to which they responded, "Mighty fine, thank ya."

The second time Randy ran into these Good Old Boys happened to be in the Food Lion supermarket in King George, Virginia. Again, Randy struck up a conversation, asking them where the best bar to listen to good country music was. His newfound friends replied, "The Eagles Nest is the best."

"Maybe I'll catch you there sometime," Randy continued, then made sure to reach the checkout line before them so that, once in the parking lot, he could note their license plate number. After he obtained information about where they lived, he assigned a team to follow these gentlemen, tracking where they went and who they encountered, despite the fact we were already running two cigarette sting operations—working with Sayid to sell the cigarettes, and following customers who were smuggling the cigarettes they'd purchased from us in Virginia back into NYC.

"You get made and you better go fucking home right then. You definitely won't be working this operation any longer," he informed the undercovers.

After a few days, surveillance gave Randy a heads-up that the Good Old Boys were on their way to Wawa (a convenience store). A smile spread across Randy's face as he jumped in the truck and arrived at Wawa, already in redneck mode in under two minutes.

"Damn, you guys are here more than me," Randy said, quick to strike up a conversation.

The Good Old Boys smiled and engaged in small talk, which led to what the boys thought was a slip-up from Randy about business partners in NYC. Randy could tell they were intrigued.

"What do you do for a living?" the tall one asked. He had a piece of beef jerky stuck in the middle of his front teeth.

"I travel for business," Randy stated, a quick comeback an undercover would have at the ready.

Eyebrows suddenly raised, a sign for Randy to keep going.

"I'm just trying to make a living. Seeing those few years I spent in prison, making a living on a regular man's salary is nearly impossible."

The Good Old Boys pushed further, trying to uncover what he did.

"You boys got time for a drink or two?" Randy laughed. "That's a long story."

Hook, line, and sinker, the boys were in. After a purchase at Wawa, the Good Old Boys led him to a bar two blocks down where only two other gentlemen sat, watching a rerun of *Gunsmoke*.

After a couple of shots, Butch, the small man who appeared to be in charge, finally led the conversation.

"So what were you really in prison for?"

"I was pulled over in Northern New York, near the Canadian border. I had ten cases of untaxed cigarettes that I'd just bought on the Akwesasne Reservation by Massena. I had a couple of priors, so on top of the smuggling cigarettes charge, they slapped me with a felony and time in prison."

"Holy shit," Zooman said. "They put you in prison for that?"

Zooman was the nickname for the muscle guy. Even though he was smaller than Butch, he was younger and in better shape.

"The attorney general and governor had a real hard on for smuggling from reservations." Randy shrugged. "It affects New York taxes and messes with their revenue, apparently. New York doesn't play when it comes to their money."

"So how was it?" Butch questioned.

"The smuggling?"

"Prison. Is it as bad as they say?" Zooman asked.

Disappointed that the boys bit on the opposite of Randy's intentions, he continued, "I was in Dannemora in the Clinton Correctional Facility, so it wasn't too bad. A bit of a mix of Hispanics and blacks, but a lot of Native Americans, too, which helped me. You know, the officers in my jail were good old country boys like you. They helped me, too. Seeing as I never gave up on anybody, my time was uneventful. Add to that a good portion of the employees ended up becoming my customers. My partner was still working on the outside, so he helped supply cigarettes for the guards."

Randy could tell by their body language they weren't ready for his pitch yet. So he used my favorite tactic and changed the subject.

"How'd you get the name Zooman?"

"Butch gave me the name."

Randy paused, afraid he might refer to a past history of a zoo or farm animal or some crazy work shit.

"Butch was a real ladies' man," Zooman explained, and he proceeded to tell a story about a beautiful redheaded woman Butch met after he'd wrecked his truck. The redhead who, Butch reminded Zooman, looked like Cybil Shepard with legs like Kathleen Turner, captured his attention. There to give a written statement and provide the police report, Butch couldn't leave without inviting her for a drink, to which she said yes.

At happy hour, Butch discovered that the redhead had a boyfriend who was married and lived in the bridle of Maryland, only a twenty-minute drive away. Seeing that Butch was married, too, the redhead having a boyfriend in place worked out perfectly. Butch knew it was only a matter of time before he got laid.

By the second happy hour, the redhead stated she was tired of her married boyfriend not leaving his wife and had told him she was going to start dating. Once the boyfriend heard her plan, he reminded her that he would not put up with her dating. Butch graciously handed her a hundred-dollar bill and told her to go out and have a good time.

By now, Randy wished Zooman's story was about farm animals. Instead, this was a never-ending story about Butch getting laid.

After she had her ladies' night out, Butch called her at the office and asked to meet again. Her boyfriend was out of town at a fireman's convention, so she offered cocktails at her house instead.

"He was a volunteer fireman for Dalgreen!" Butch exclaimed. "And a prison guard in Waverly, Virginia, for the state on the insert team. He was one of those crazy-ass bastards who go into the cell and drag out violent offenders."

"Butch has a good friend in the carpet and furniture business," Zooman interjected.

"For God's sake, please tell me where the end of this story leads." Randy sighed.

"We're coming to the good part," Butch said.

Zooman resumed telling the story, "While he was hitting it for the second time, thinking gorgeous was the best sex he'd ever had, there was a knock at the door. While Butch was tripping over himself to put his pants on, she gave him a big smile. The knock was a flower delivery from the boyfriend with a card that read: "Let's get together when I get back."

Well, Butch was half dressed with a soft dick. But Red said, "You're not leaving."

"Damn right I am," he said. "This guy is still interested in you, and I don't ever want to meet him."

"Great story, but it's time for my story," Randy said.

"No!" Butch said. "Here comes the part where I became Zooman."

"I'm only listening if you end this bullshit now."

Butch continued. "A couple of years pass, and I take my kids to the zoo, and who is there volunteering that week but Red? She says hi and asks me how I've been. I tell her my house burned down and we're in the process of building a new one. I jokingly ask, 'You don't think your boyfriend had anything to do with my house burning down, do you?'"

"'Could be,' she said. 'Just another reason I dumped him and had an order of protection against him.'

"Anyway, after a couple of visits to the zoo and having coffee with her, I tell her some bullshit story about how well I'm doing in the trucking business. Suddenly, she wants to meet me at her friend's apartment. Even though she has an order of protection against the boyfriend, I feel better meeting her at her friend's apartment. But after twenty minutes, even though she's beautiful, I cannot get hard. Even after we take a shower. I like to think it was because of the boyfriend."

"Hold on, is this whole story about you not getting laid? You are one dumb motherfucker," Randy stated.

"Well, you asked why my name was Zooman."

"You do realize that name is not a compliment?"

Butch, who'd been snickering throughout the torturous story, finally let out one of the biggest laughs Randy had ever heard.

Randy told me later, "If these two motherfuckers buy cigarettes, I'm personally cuffing them and telling this boyfriend what jail they're in before they're transported." Be advised,

Randy was also a volunteer fireman besides being a hard-ass cop.

Once he had them on cigarette smuggling and told them all their assets would be seized, including their cars and businesses, they were devastated. As promised, he also let Butch and Zooman know that he told his fellow volunteer firemen who they were and where they were being held so the crazy boyfriend could find them. The two men cried like girls.

Beyond the Good Old Boys, "Randy Redneck" never worked undercover in Virginia, but the name stuck, and he did make a cameo appearance in a few New York and New Jersey operations.

Besides the danger that comes from our line of work comes the patience and perseverance we have to show to make the bad guys feel comfortable. Trust is the strongest asset an undercover has. It's only after the bad guys trust you that they allow greed to take over. Then the arrest is only a matter of time.

[11]

EL BOBBO HELD HOSTAGE!

Okay, this is not as bad as it sounds. Well, at least initially. It did get a hell of a lot more intense as the hours passed.

It all started when El Bobbo was making cig deliveries in Harlem. As most undercovers did, El Bobbo had criminals who would only work with a specific type of individual. For example, Arabs will only work with other Arabs. El Bobbo was that type with Malik, our target.

El Bobbo had done the first few deliveries with Sayid, our informant. In case you have not read my first book, *Under Too Long*, these criminals will cheat anybody, especially other crooks.

So Malik talked to El Bobbo about getting rid of his guy, Sayid, as the middleman and dealing directly with El Bobbo.

El Bobbo portrayed himself as a big dumb moron, always making mistakes with deliveries and the money count, which

Malik fell for hook, line, and sinker. El Bobbo was a damn good undercover, and bad guys ate this shit up.

El Bobbo was one smart bastard. He actually graduated from the same college I did, though twenty-plus years after me. My "*son* from another mother" was six foot five, athletic, and definitely an agent you wanted with you in dangerous situations.

Like El Bobbo, Jeff was another agent who you wanted with you when the shit hit the fan.

There were numerous other agents I felt the same way about. But Jeff and El Bobbo and I had a special bond—Jeff because he was in the room with me when the Africans drew weapons, and El Bobbo when I had a gun put to the back of my head.

A bond that will exist till the day we die.

So here's my fuck up.

After Malik convinced El Bobbo to do private deals without Sayid, I broke one of the rules of undercover ops, and made the call to let El Bobbo make deliveries alone. I justified this because we would have two backup vehicles and he would be wearing a wire.

Also, Malik was El Bobbo's long-time customer, and Malik stood by his word. He would only deal with El Bobbo alone. We called his bluff, we thought, on the first delivery, and went in with a team. It was about ten minutes after El Bobbo arrived at the meet in Brooklyn. Malik was so paranoid about running into Sayid in Harlem he wanted to do deals in Brooklyn. So El Bobbo pulled up to the location near a funeral parking lot at the corner of Flatbush on East 123rd, if I remember correctly.

Ten minutes after El Bobbo pulled up, Malik called and told El Bobbo, in his broken English, "I no meet," and hung up. El Bobbo called him back, but Malik did not answer. So we packed it in. Seeing we were all tired from being up for twenty hours, we said, "Fuck it, we'll worry about it tomorrow."

Around four a.m. the next day, El Bobbo decided that since the primary undercover always had the final say, he thought, *Fuck him, that greedy bastard will call when he needs more cases of cigarettes.*

Sure enough, Malik called two days later and said he needed more cigs. Because he had lost money for the two days he did not have cigs, he wanted a better deal. Instead of $2,300 per case, he said he would only pay $2,000. El Bobbo said, and I quote, "Listen, you slimy weasel fuck, the price is $2,300, and if you don't want them, you can go and fuck yourself and those thirteen girls you dream about," making reference to terrorists' beliefs that when they died and saw whomever, they would have thirteen virgins waiting for them.

Malik caved on the price but demanded El Bobbo show up alone. El Bobbo agreed. Then he told us, "Let's get a few more deals on him, have him arrested, and we'll be done with this fucking weasel."

After a couple more deals, we felt safe and decided to go for two more before arresting him and throwing him in jail to see how soon he shit himself.

Not sure if it was due to Murphy's Law—whatever could go wrong would go wrong—or that we had become complacent with all the deliveries in this op coming off without any issues, but it all changed with the next delivery. El Bobbo was wired. We had two backup vehicles, one on each end of a side street/alleyway off East 123rd Street.

Malik pulled up to El Bobbo, and started telling him something that was hard to understand because Malik was talking fast in that broken English of his. Plus, the reception on our end was lousy because of the buildings that enclosed this alleyway.

Within minutes, Malik, with El Bobbo following, flew by the vehicle at the south end of the alleyway. Our trail vehicle did follow them but lost them in traffic within minutes, which was common in New York City where half of the drivers disobeyed traffic laws, and stopped, parked, and exited their vehicle at random. Murphy's Law One.

The reception got worse on our bug and eventually died completely. Murphy's Law Two.

Unknown to us, El Bobbo was unaware we'd lost him and were not picking up his transmission. After an hour went by where everybody on the detail was blaming each other for this fuckup, my phone rang and El Bobbo was on the other end. Before he could say another word, Malik had the phone and told me he wanted his price of $2,000 per case. "And you will not see your man El Bobbo until you agree to my price," he added.

I'm not sure if I was so pissed at what occurred and all the bullshit going on, but I told Malik, "Fuck *you* and fuck that idiot El Bobbo. I'll just get another idiot to make deliveries!" And I hung up! Well, every agent in the warehouse was staring at me with a look of *what the fuck?* They had no way of knowing what El Bobbo said on his end that led to that kind of reaction from me. Of course, Billy the Liquor Guy always knew what to say.

Yeah, right!

I blurted out to my team that Malik was a businessman and we would negotiate the price, but I questioned whether this was true.

Finally, I told everyone to shut the fuck up and calm down. I knew everyone was pissed at me, so I asked Randy C., Jeff Who, Brihiem, and Nick at Night what we should do. I also asked the Deer Slayer, but as usual, he just kept staring into space.

Randy C., who definitely was the smartest man in the room, said, "Let's wait a while so we don't look weak. Then we'll call and say we will cut the price in half to $1,150, and tell him that it's the best we can do due to our costs on this particular deal. But in future deals, we would consider $2,000."

I was guessing every agent in the room was thinking this was Malik's last deal, one way or another.

I remembered the incident from an arrest of the terrorist who had a ticket from the World Trade Center Observation Deck dated September 10th, the day before the Towers went down. Rumor was he tripped down the stairs of his second-floor apartment *twice*.

Two hours went by, which seemed like ten. I made the call to El Bobbo's phone, and after about twenty minutes of negotiating with Malik, and him screaming and shouting, I had done all I could do not to hang up on him again. But thank God a deal was made, and we agreed to a location to make the swap.

Well, what happened next was surreal.

Malik showed up with two other Arabs. Jeff Who and I met them. Randy C., with a team of agents, was secreted in the area. Well, within seconds, Malik and his crew, and Jeff Who and I, as well as El Bobbo all had red laser dots all over our bodies. El Bobbo said, in his fake Polish accent, "Billy, what we do?"

Well, Jeff Who, always the one to make a joke, said, very calmly, "I would definitely not run!"

Meanwhile, Malik and his crew were speaking in their high-pitched dialect. Within seconds, we were surrounded by a NYC SWAT Team screaming, "Get down, get down! Any sudden moves, we will shoot!"

While lying on the ground, Randy C., always the smartest guy in any room, approached the scene with a couple of unmarked cars with red lights and sirens, after identifying himself on the radio to NYC SWAT Team.

As Randy approached this clusterfuck scene, he explained to the team leader of the SWAT Team who we were and that we were performing a cigarette sting operation, but did not mention the kidnapping.

Thank God, eventually, it was agreed the SWAT Team would take in Malik and his crew while Randy and his team of Petroleum, Alcohol and Tobacco agents would take in the other idiots—us. Of course, they hooked us up and threw us into the back seat of the PATB op vehicle too. Pretty fucking roughly, I thought.

Oh well, I guess this was the buildup from the past few days' tension.

To end on a note of levity, while sitting in the back of the police vehicle, El Bobbo asked me, "Did you really tell Malik to fuck himself and me?"

Jeff Who said to El Bobbo, "This was all your fault, you dumb bastard."

Then El Bobbo and Jeff Who started bumping into each other and yelling things like "When I get these handcuffs off, I'm going to beat the balls off you!"

Once we exited the scene, I asked Randy to pull over and take the handcuffs off. Randy's reply? "Maybe when we get to the warehouse. What I should do is leave them on and put you all in a cell, you dumb bastards."

[12]
PEOPLE YOU MEET

I realize that, in our lifetime, we meet many people. If we're lucky, people of different ethnicities and backgrounds—rich and poor, educated and some not so much—cross our lives. Personally, I prefer down-to-earth, blue collar, ordinary folk.

My mom was good about allowing me to bring home friends she would otherwise call "street persons." I cannot count the number of times we played "guess who's coming to dinner." But that was during the 1950s and '60s when times were different.

I know now that my childhood was a building block to becoming a damn good undercover agent. It was something I never understood or absorbed, but I would get these feelings of confidence and self-assurance whenever I was around people who others would call less fortunate. I enjoyed my time with these individuals and felt at ease when I was around them.

My mom used to joke that I could talk to a homeless person as well as I could talk to a bank president. Who knew years later that I'd discover her statement was right. It's been years since my mother said those words to me, yet I've had my fair share of conversations with millionaires and homeless individuals, all with the same caliber of intent—which might validate my mother's other saying that I was born with the right initials: B.S.

One of the things I enjoyed as an undercover was the opportunity to meet and interact with an even wider range of individuals, from mafia hitmen to high-ranking politicians to my share of well-known actors and sports figures. Mind you, these were all short encounters, but they were all valuable, nonetheless.

For example, due to my gold shield and the help of the NYPD, I met Mariano Rivera, Derek Jeter, and A-Rod (Alex Rodriguez). I may or may not have pushed a twelve-year-old kid out of the way so I could shake Rivera's hand, which felt a lot like sandpaper.

The first person I encountered during my undercover career who I considered to be famous was Jeanine Pirro. At the time, Ms. Pirro was the District Attorney for Westchester County, which encompassed a large portion of my undercover area. The team I was assigned to had completed a huge bust, which included cigarettes, drugs, guns, and a nice chunk of money from the bad guys.

District Attorney Pirro commanded attention just through the confidence she held as she addressed various law enforcement agencies. What impressed me the most was the enthusiasm she demonstrated for bringing dangerous criminals to justice. Also, after press conferences, Pirro took the time to thank every agent in the room individually.

BEN STILLER

Ben Stiller is a great, down-to-earth guy. I was at my favorite bar in Plattsburg, NY when I noticed the owner, Bobbi Hall, had gone down the hall to greet a man I immediately knew was Ben Stiller—unless he had a twin. Bobbi Hall started greeting multiple people who just kept filing into the bar. I watched as Stiller went behind the bar and began looking around. I'd been aware that Ben was in town filming the miniseries *Escape at Dannemora*. In fact, Bobbi had already met Stiller's sister, who'd scouted the bar for a spot in the film.

Even though I was now retired, my Billy the Liquor Guy mode found its way out. I began razzing with Ben.

"Well, I assume you're the new bartender we've been waiting on. Can I get a screwdriver?" I was playing like I had no idea who he was. "You look a little lost back there," I teased.

"Thank you," Ben joked, which gave me the nudge to play this out, even when the assistant director approached me and advised me I had to leave.

"He's staying!" Bobbi shot back.

I ignored the annoyed director who sighed and walked away as Ben continued to examine the bar lighting.

"Hope this doesn't mean I can't get another drink." I laughed.

Ben looked up at me, smiled, and said, "I'll get you." Stiller began pouring vodka into a glass.

"I've never seen the bar this crowded before," I remarked. "What's going on?"

"Sir, we're trying to shoot a scene here for a movie," the assistant director replied. "So unless you want to be in the movie, we need you to move so we can work."

I looked at the director in annoyance. "I'm probably the one guy in this damn city that does not want to be in this movie," I said loud enough for Ben to hear.

Bobbi gave me the evil eye, while Stiller looked at me inquisitively.

"You know, your dad was one funny bastard, and you're not so bad either," I said to him. "I'm sorry for your loss, by the way. I enjoyed your dad's career for a long time. He made a lot of people laugh. From what I've heard, your dad was a really nice guy." Ben smiled and handed me the drink.

"I've heard you're just like your dad in that regard. I'm a big fan of your work, too."

"Thought you didn't know who I was," Stiller joked.

"Ah, I had to play with you a little bit."

"You know who this is?" Bobbi interjected, referring to me. "This is a great undercover who did a lot for our state. He's one of our local heroes. In fact, he's writing a book now [my first book, *Undercover Too Long*] about his time undercover."

I placed my hand on Stiller's shoulder as Bobbi continued to sing my praises. Then I cracked, "Ben, if this thing you're doing doesn't work out, I'll send you my book and maybe we can do something together."

"Sounds good, sir," Stiller said.

I saw him a few more times in the bar. We talked about work, Dannemora prison, and life in New York City. My initial judgment was correct. He was a good guy, someone who related well with people.

HITMEN

Among the bad guys who built my career were the hitmen I came across. It began with my grandfather, who everyone referred to as "a soldier." A soldier in Italian is Soldato, so you can imagine my thoughts as a seven-year-old boy.

Did that mean all Soldatos are hitmen? I wondered.

"Are we hitmen?" I asked my grandfather.

My grandfather put a huge smile on his face, which rarely happened, and gave me a big hug. Then he pulled me back and looked me in the eyes.

"No, Billy. You're not, and your father definitely is not."

"What about you, Grandpa?"

"I am a soldier. I do what they tell me."

And that was it. We never discussed the topic again. While I often wondered how many other soldiers and hitmen I stood beside as I grew up, I knew for a fact that one particular experience was enough to keep me away from wondering about hitmen altogether.

It was October 1976. I was 23 and had moved back home to save money. I was up watching television at my parents' house on Rugar Street when I heard a number of gunshots coming from my parents' backyard. This was not the first time I'd heard gunshots, but I'd never heard them this close to my house.

I immediately hit the ground. My heart was pounding against the cold wooden floor as I waited. The sound of screeching tires flying down the street behind my house followed, then soon the sound of police sirens. I got up enough courage to crawl to the back window and peek out. I could see multiple police cars lining Rugar Street, which was less than fifty yards away.

The smart thing would have been to stay in my house, but being me, I followed that other voice and went to check it out. I put my dog on a leash and walked over to the area behind my house.

"Nothing to see here," a police officer responded as I walked past.

But there was something to see: a dead guy in a blue suit with bullet holes all over his body.

"Billy?" one of the young cops questioned before I was shooed away. He was one of my high school buddies who I'd also taken a criminal justice course with at the local community college.

"Sergeant, this is the chief of police's nephew," he said, which happened to be true. "He could be a witness as that's his house."

The sergeant looked from the house he was pointing at to me. "You see anything, kid?"

"I heard a couple of shots, but I didn't see anything," I replied.

At this time in Utica, not too many witnesses came forward. And, even if I had seen something, my grandfather's voice echoed in my head: *"Never get involved! Never offer information, and never, ever testify in court against family, friends, or made members of the mob. You got that?!"*

As if on cue, the guy on the sidewalk began stirring,

choking on his blood. I don't know if the cops were as surprised as me to realize the man was alive, but their attention quickly diverted to him, and I got out of there. As I turned to pull my dog along, I realized she'd been standing there licking the blood off the sidewalk.

Who would have thought twenty-five years later I'd be hired as a hitman? I think I pulled it off pretty well in my undercover role. Actually, it sometimes worked too well. Yeah, and\ old friend tried to hire me to kill someone. She thought Billy the Liquor Guy was real. I played along for a while, trying to find out more. But I was getting too involved. I reported it to the cops and walked away from it.

R.G.

A more up-close-and-personal contact with a hitman occurred last November. I was invited to a P.B. & J Italian breakfast. Yes, P.B. & J does mean peanut butter and jelly, but for Italians, it means all the fixings too: sausage and peppers, meatballs, tomato pie, macaroni, and so much more. And wine, of course.

R.G. was an old friend from East Utica, who happened to have mafia connections. R.G. had set up the breakfast so that this hitman could meet me. How the hell R.G. found me is still a mystery to me, seeing as I hadn't seen him in over forty years. But I knew better than to ask. R.G. said he wanted me to meet one of my grandfather's associates who helped my grandfather when he was in and out of prison.

So, at this breakfast, the hitman, now in his 80s, wanted to tell me that my grandfather was a stand up guy, and that he'd be turning over in his grave if he knew I made a living arresting bad guys.

He started with, "Kid, you know who I am?"

"Yes, sir," I replied. This was a made man who'd spent half his life in prison.

"I knew your grandfather," he said. "He was a stand-up guy. He did two terms of prison for the nephew of my boss." The story goes that the nephew whined to his uncle that he had left his jacket at the business he'd just robbed—his wallet was in the pocket—and he just could not do time in prison. His uncle, who people ironically called Big Joe, even though he was only five foot six, was the "Godfather" of Utica. He ran part of Upstate's mob and was one of the heads at the Appalachian meeting in 1957, which was attended by over one hundred La Cosa Nostra bosses.

The second time he was part of an arrest for bootlegging. Big Joe reached out to my grandfather, who agreed to testify that the booze this nephew had embezzled was in fact his. The nephew was given a new line of work soon after, and we didn't hear much from him after that.

My grandfather had left Sicily beside his father, who was fleeing because he was unwilling to pay protection to keep his family safe there. He came to America for a new life.

The last thing I ever wanted to be was a cop. I always preferred my grandfather's life. But life takes many twists and turns. I always liked to figure out crimes. That's not to say I didn't plan a few in my head, my favorite being my fantasy of hijacking a Fargo armored vehicle loaded with money and making my escape via helicopter. This was a fun fantasy for a 23-year-old.

After he said, "Your grandfather's probably turning over in his grave knowing you became law enforcement," I said, "No disrespect, sir, but I'm quite familiar how the family handles things. When someone hurts your family you do whatever you can to take them down. I work as a cop on behalf of my 40 friends who were lost in 9/11."

I was proud to grow up in East Utica in the 1950s and '60. The mafia I knew only went after people who were trying to kill them or threaten the livelihood of their families. Most of the soldiers I knew were born into the lifestyle.

The hitman, whom I'll call Mr. D, asked me, "Did you have $368,000 worth of cash sitting between you and another agent, from what I've heard?"

"Yes, sir."

"Why didn't you just take it?"

In my quick, Billy-the-Liquor-Guy wit, I said, "Not enough money to change your life for all the hiding I'd have to do."

"It would have been a start," Mr. D said.

"Not really. Plus, I was with a coworker."

He looked me dead in the eye. "So why not shoot him?" he asked, as smooth as if he were ordering a coffee.

"He's a good friend." I shrugged, attempting to make light of the conversation.

"You have no friends when it involves hundreds of thousands of dollars."

"Like I said," I said, trying to change the subject, as I was spooked, "my targets were terrorists from September 11th. My focus was only on them. Growing up in East Utica when streets were safe, back when every Baby Boomer grew up knowing the mafia and the way of life, I saw when times were changing, so I put my education on the streets, especially the Boulevard of Broken Dreams, to catch the real bad guys."

"Okay, kid. You made your case. But I still disagree with you. You should have taken the money."

"So we agree to disagree," I joked, my heart racing.

"Yeah, well, your grandfather was a stand-up guy. He never squealed."

"As were you. That's why you did twenty-seven years." Before I exited the room, I turned to Mr. D one last time. "By the way, I have a price, and it has six zeros that come after a crooked number."

"Well, kid, if you come across that before I die and go to Hell, you call me and I'll be there—and no one will even have to die. That you'll have my word on."

Most of the guys from the three-block radius where I grew up ended up dead or in jail. Very few came out unscathed, on the side of the law, like the Mayor of Utica… and me.

ATTORNEY GENERAL ANDREW CUOMO

Andrew Cuomo. Or, as I referred to him in *Under Too Long*, The General.

If you had a chance to listen to the audio version, you would have heard how psyched I was to meet him and be assigned to his task force, even though it was pure luck that I walked into the Soft Tail Bar in Elmira, NY.

I still have flashbacks of meeting Elephant Man, the supposed owner of the bar. But you can read all about that in the first book, *Under too Long*. And I hope you will!

Luck or not, once I heard from Tom Stanton, waking me up the next day at zero dark hundred, he explained to me that our Operation Spirits had fallen into the attorney general's "Thunder and Lightning" narcotics op. Of course, my team was able to take down the Soft Tail Bar for drugs when Cuomo's task force had three different sets of undercovers thrown out on their respective asses.

I was thinking this could be huge. Especially when Mr. Cuomo walked into the room and broke Tony's and my balls. Then the attorney general's right-hand man and a couple of his assistants kept peppering me with questions, like, "How the hell did you get so close to this perp, and within only your second contact, like you were lifelong friends?"

As excited as I was, I went into my Billy the Liquor Guy routine of throwing out a line of bullshit. My response was, "Like the attorney general said, I am a large old white-haired guy and Tony (my partner) does look like an accountant."

Basically, we looked harmless and definitely didn't look like cops. But we did know the liquor business. Having actually owned a bar, I could bullshit with the best of them. And I was somewhat aware of the illegal activity that could occur in the bar business. Plus, Tony was a very smart businessman.

The attorney general just smiled and said, "Maybe I do have the right team," and exited the room.

This was when Cuomo's right-hand man stated that Tony and I were being assigned to the attorney general's task force and would be given anything we needed: cars, manpower, state-of-the-art listening and surveillance equipment, etc.

If you heard the audiobook, I sounded like a kid at Christmas, laughing and blurting out, "Tony, you believe this shit?

We're working for the fucking attorney general." Not very professional, but I knew this was the opportunity of a lifetime. And I was going to make the most of it.

To be honest, I saw Mr. Cuomo very little during the op. But I did have multiple notices from high-ranking officials about how happy the attorney general was.

Once Thunder and Lightning concluded, there was a press conference, which was in New York City or Albany, I forget. It made the TV and newspapers and was labeled the largest drugs, illegal cigs, and alcohol and weapons bust ever. I've only heard this, 'cause I'm not much of a reader, so I've never researched it. If you're curious, you could look up Operation Thunder and Lightning, New York State Attorney General's Office.

Anyway, from working for the attorney general for a large part of my undercover career, I can say Andrew Cuomo's number one interest was New York State. He was smart, had a set of balls, and did not take excuses from anybody working for him. Just get it done was his attitude.

Being an Italian who did not take any bullshit myself, I felt it a privilege to work from him. I'm sure some people might condemn me for praising him or maybe call it sucking up to some idiots. My guess is these are people that never accomplished anything and are good at complaining, but they never come up with a solution. To them, I'd say, "You would be lucky to have anything close to his drive and the care he has for New York State." As far as sucking up, I am old, retired, and content with my life, and I don't need or want anything.

And Mr. Cuomo doesn't need me to defend or support him.

One thing to note. After Thunder and Lightning, my identity was "intentionally" given out in a media article. Here's the scene: Double J, the guy we took down, was being interviewed by state police personnel, and all was going well. They were treating him respectfully and he was responding nicely.

Like I said, the interview was going well, but I guess not fast enough. So this "suit"—some tech guy who thought he was a big macher and appointed himself the liaison between Double J and me and Cuomo's task force. Anyway, the guy suddenly rushed into the room and told Double J, "You think you're so street smart, but that Liquor Guy you sold all those drugs to was an undercover agent." I was told Big Ed "escorted" this suit—who never worked a day in the streets and was a political appointment—out immediately.

Well, Big Ed went up one side and down another with this suit, and I was told that all you heard was this guy apologizing over and over. I was not there, but a rumor went around that he pissed his pants.

[PART 4]
A DAY OFF...

[13]
DEKE, MY MAN!

During a book tour of the Carolinas, while I was in South Carolina, I took a day off to write this second book near the ocean.

I found a cabana bar, advertising the "Best Turkey Burger in Charleston, SC." I pulled into the parking lot with my pad and a copy of my *Under Too Long* book for reference. I picked out a picnic table with an umbrella. Next to me there were half a dozen women celebrating a birthday.

Sure enough, within five minutes of setting my book, *Under Too Long*, in plain view of the ladies, one asked, "Are you reading or writing?"

My response was, "Both. I'm working on my second book."

Her response, as usual, was, "You wrote a book?"

"Yes."

"What's it's about?"

"My undercover career."

I not only sold a few books to them, but other patrons started lining up. Before I knew it, I had sold an additional twelve books.

When I went to pay my bill, the birthday party ladies paid my tab! The waitress said the ladies told her about my book, and she told her boss Deke, and he wanted to talk to me.

Deke asked me, "What you drinking?"

I thought, *At least I'm getting a drink before he bitches to me about selling books at his place and throws me out.* To my surprise, it was the complete opposite.

Deke told me, "I just checked out your book on Amazon." He added he was a true crime fan and said it looked interesting. Going into Billy the Liquor Guy sales mode, I pulled a hardcover book out of my work bag, signed it, and gave it to him in appreciation of the Best Turkey Burger in Charleston!

Within a few minutes, we connected. He was military. Just by his demeanor and confidence, I knew Deke had seen his share of action. It helped that he added that he was out of country for most of his sixteen-plus years, all over the world, for Army Delta Force/Special Ops.

Now I was hooked, seeing I'd never served but had listened to the war stories from family and friends that did, from WWII, the Korean War, and Vietnam. Like most vets who been in battle, at first Deke did not talk that much about what he'd seen. Eventually, I told him I had to leave, but I'd come back tomorrow so we could do lunch.

Deke said, "Sounds good."

The next day, Deke said, "I read your book, or most of it."

I thanked him and said it meant a lot to me coming from a special ops soldier who'd been in a hell of lot more danger than me. Deke said, "Whether you fight battles in the jungles or on concrete, we've all paid our dues."

Well, after lunch and drinks that led into happy hour, Deke said, "We have a big happy hour tomorrow. If it's okay with you, I'll have a little promotion for you and tell all my military buddies and cops about it."

"Of course," I said. "Sounds good," even though, after hearing whatever he could tell me about his ops, I still felt like my UC work was like child's play to these vets.

But just like my support groups with mostly vets, the vets I met the next day made me feel like I was part of a brotherhood.

Especially when a SEAL Team 5 member said, "Yes, we face danger, but only periodically, and we're prepared before we go into harm's way. You are in danger every minute, never knowing when your situation can turn into shit within a second."

Even though I did not agree, it did pump me up. Primarily because I now was included in this Band of Brothers who did their best to make our country safe. This made it a bit easier, again realizing what we did was worth it.

Although this feeling took years to realize, to this day, when my PTSD hits me hard, when I have flashbacks of the death of friends due to 9/11 and see the shit I saw from that day as well as in my undercover career, I do question, was it really worth it?

What works for me, when I am alone and going down that black hole of despair, is listening to songs that help me back to reality. Don't laugh, my favorite is "Red River Valley," which I danced for the father/daughter dance at my daughter's wedding. I'm listening to it right now! What also helps is, because I live in the Northeast, jumping in a lake or pool, any month of the year. Lake ice is thin near shore. Or I'll find a support group to get to or talk to somebody who has been there dealing with PTSD.

That's why I connected so well with Deke, so much so that I ended up staying in the Charlestown, SC area for three weeks. Deke hooked me up with a place to stay.

One of my brothers in arms who Deke introduced me to was a SEAL Team 5 member, Kurt Muse. John Gilstrap wrote a book about him, *Six Minutes to Freedom*. One of the stories in the book was about when his unit rescued a civilian, who was a journalist. This was the first time an op was to rescue a civilian. The journalist had been abducted by Noriega's drug cartel. Kurt Muse was rescued, and the rescue was eventually made into a couple of movies. Kurt gave my book to his author, who thought highly of it, and we set up a meeting while I was in the Carolinas.

When it was determined that Gilstrap had two books in progress and was going to be in Europe, Deke put me in touch with Jeffrey Deaver. Both of these authors have written multiple bestsellers.

Again, it is nothing until it is something. But it sure feels good to be recognized! After contacting these two authors, *Under Too Long* was listed on Amazon along with James Patterson, Gilstrap, Deaver, Ben MacIntyre, and Gregory Freeman's book, *The Forgotten 500*, about the men who risked it all for the greatest rescue mission of World War II. Pretty good company.

In the last few years, Deke has become a good friend who has helped me with my PTSD.

Thank you, Deke, for your friendship and support! From day one, you accepted me into your group of heroes who fought all over the world. Hope to see you again soon, my brother in arms.

[14]
TUXEDO BOY

There are a few things I've seen in life that make me say "now, there's something you don't see every day." Meeting Tuxedo Boy was one of those moments. I was in a hotel in Virginia, swimming laps. Though my favorite childhood and adult activities seemed to gradually evolve from swimming in lakes and ponds to pools, it was still one of the regimented activities I clung to.

Swimming had been one of my constants in life. It has had so much to do with my healing process from PTSD, and had so much to do with my childhood. In my youth, I could swim faster than all my friends who, I must admit, were all more athletic than me. As I was a chubbier kid who weighed more than my brother and my cousin put together, it felt great to beat them in the water. I'd tread water deeper and longer than any of my siblings or friends, thinking of the names they'd proudly given me: whale, chubby bastard and, a popular public comment from my brother to this day, "God, you're huge!"

Just as in our later life, my cousin Joe always helped me out. During my struggle with PTSD, that help came back around. As a former serviceman in Vietnam, he saw more than his fair share of death—including an incident for which he's still awaiting his Purple Heart. For someone who saw so much up close and personal, his talks helped pull me through. I can still hear him say, "You can do this," when times get tough and I second-guess my actions. But my brother Frank (who is 16 months older than me), well, I just beat the balls off him now. Just kidding, but ever since he got out of the Navy, he's remained a skinny fuck, whereas I became a lot stronger.

Whenever we were in a pool, where I could catch him, I'd hold him underwater until I knew he'd had enough. Of course, the second I'd let him up, he'd say, "You fat bastard. You're still huge, you know."

My brother is a smart bastard—on paper. He graduated from nuke school—he trained as a nuclear technician in the Navy—and went on to operate nuclear submarines for six years. Yet, in my eyes, he's still an idiot. I remember when we were looking at pictures after my mother's funeral, and a photo of myself at the prom with our grandfather by my side, came up. "Was Poppi alive then?" my brother asked. I just looked at the photo again and shook my head.

Hours later, he fell into my mother's graveside, which was covered by a tarp and had a large sign that read "Do Not Walk On." The best part was he never spilled his drink.

On our cross-country trip, where we drove his daughter's car from New York to Seattle, we stopped at Mount Rushmore. It was majestic, with designated viewing posts that were custom at all national parks. However, these viewing posts weren't close enough for my brother. So he decided to climb over the fence, which clearly read "No Admittance."

"You're an idiot," I said as I left him and walked back to the car.

Of course, within minutes, I heard all the bells and whistles before he came running back to the car, yelling, "Holy shit, they're serious about that shit. Go!"

I actually hoped the federal park rangers would chase us down as we drove away.

By the time we were passing through Montana, he took a break from his daydreaming out the window and looked over at me, as if something important had just crossed his mind.

"You were a cop?"

"Yes," I replied.

"Did they give you a gun?"

"Yes."

"Handcuffs, too?"

"Yes."

"You ever shoot anybody?"

"Not until today."

"You wrote a book about it?"

"Yes."

"Did you die in the book?"

"Frank! It's a true story!"

"Okay, but did you die?"

"Yeah, I died and my ghost is driving this car."

To all the people who live near a nuclear power plant in Connecticut, which my brother has run for years alongside other nuclear technicians who look like the Unabomber, good luck to you!

Back in Virginia, I was swimming at a local Marriot when a middle-aged gentleman carrying a tuxedo walked into the pool area. I peered at him through my goggles, wondering where this gentleman was going with a tuxedo in his hand and a bathing suit on.

"I didn't know this was a formal pool party," I joked as the man hung up his tux and headed toward the pool.

Well, this Billy Joel lookalike just ignored me. But he reminded me of my good friend Johnny Gazzal for some odd reason, so I tried again.

"How you doing?" I asked.

Again, the middle-aged tuxedo man ignored me. Clearly, he was an asshole. So I tightened my goggles and started swimming again, determined to kick his ass in the water. Once he began to do his laps, I picked up my pace. I passed him again and again, my competitive angle dispelling the anger and irritation I felt toward his dismissal.

After I passed him numerous times, I happily stepped out of the pool, pleased with my workout. I'll admit it wasn't a large pool; however, when you're six feet and chubby, you take any athletic wins you can get. I turned my back to him, pretending to towel off so he couldn't see me struggling to catch my breath. To my right was a redheaded woman who'd been doing water aerobics.

"I never saw anyone swim that fast in such a small pool." She laughed.

"Just trying to work out some anger issues."

"Oh, dear," she responded, which signaled a Billy the

Liquor Guy sales pitch. Only, before I could tell her about my book, Tuxedo Boy walked out of the pool and approached us.

"Do either of you have any idea where I can find a high-end restaurant to have a good meal in?" I picked up on his Middle Eastern dialect and the fact that his question was centered on the Kathleen Turner redhead. Yes, I have a habit of thinking everyone looks like someone.

Neither of us acknowledged the restaurant remark.

"I have to ask whose tuxedo is that? I've never seen a tuxedo poolside," the redhead joked.

"It's mine." Tuxedo Boy proudly smiled. "I just left Governor Youngkin's victory party. I'm his finance manager."

He's a bigger asshole than I thought, I noted.

"I'm flying back to Israel tomorrow. I've been here exploring the real estate."

Like a bear to honey, I was immediately drawn in.

"We've purchased half of Virginia as it is. We're looking to move into the other half," he continued.

The redhead said, "That sounds fun. I'm just a simple executive agent for an insurance firm." She shrugged, then said to me, "What about you, swimmer? Any real estate knowledge?"

"Nope. I wrote a book about my undercover career that a ghostwriter made legible."

"Undercover, that had to be dangerous," the redhead stated.

"Hence why the book is about my battle with PTSD."

"One of my coworkers has been telling me about a book like that, called *Under Too Long*. Is that you?"

"It is."

"What agency do you work for?" Tuxedo Boy jumped in.

"Once the Towers went down, I volunteered for a terrorism task force and worked for multiple agencies."

"So not the CIA." Tuxedo Boy laughed.

"What are you doing again in the U.S.?" I asked with a straight face.

Tuxedo Boy began backtracking, listing other reasons why he was in the U.S. "I guess I probably shouldn't be talking to you," he joked.

"Why would you think you shouldn't be talking to me?" I asked. The redhead was watching us closely. "It's not because all of these millions you're investing are for illegal purposes, is it?"

"Um, my friend said she could not put your book down," the redhead nervously interjected. "Did you really go to Africa to chase down bad guys?"

"Yes, but mostly to get information on our current terrorist activities."

Tuxedo Boy quietly backed up and slid back into the pool, where he began swimming laps. Keen to the actions of others, I was quick to understand he was trying to deflect our conversation and remove himself from my presence until he could slip away. I'd definitely touched a nerve, which made me consider sitting on a chair to see how long he'd sweat it out. Luckily for him, I had other obligations that evening.

"Tell you what," I said to the redhead as I left, "I'll leave you a copy of my book at the front desk."

As promised, I left a signed copy for the redhead, and she left a note for me upon checkout: *You should have stayed longer. The tuxedo guy showed me a picture of him and John Clapper and Yassir Arafat.*

Yassir, also known as Mohammad Abdal-Ra-Ufal-Qudwah-Al-Husayuia, or Abu-Ammar, was the President of the Palestinian Authority and Chairman of the Palestinian Liberation Organization Community, known as the PLO, from 1969–2004.

Damn, I guess my instincts are still correct, I told myself. *I should have stuck around for a very interesting conversation.*

[PART 5]
BACK TO WORK…

[15]

"NOW YOU'RE ANGRY"

Obviously working undercover is dangerous and very stressful. Along with being very tedious. Especially the tedious part, seeing it includes lots of waiting for the shit to hit the fan, ready to react with weapons drawn.

Jeff Who was the most stable of us. He was constantly adding a calming down effect with his humor.

We also had more than a few occasions where we were all at each other's throats, whether someone lost the target vehicle on a surveillance, an equipment breakdown, an occasional vehicle accident, or Billy the Liquor Guy going off script!

This occurred a lot. Especially the latter one. Add to that spending hours in a warehouse in mid-July and August in Virginia, sweating your ass off. Or doing a surveillance in New York dealing with freezing temps and not being able to use the heater in the car so not to be detected with a running vehicle.

El Bobbo and Jeff went at it a lot. El Bobbo was secondary UC, and Jeff was responsible for his safety. El Bobbo, like me, always changed the op while in progress. Note: Good UCs have to do this constantly.

The first time Jeff used his calming humor it was directed to me.

After a ten-hour operation, loading and unloading over two hundred cases of cigs, first from a cig distributor in Jersey, then in sweltering heat in Dahlgren, VA, I just lost it.

Cig sales were bad that day, so we had close to one hundred cases left to reload back into the truck. Each case weighed sixty pounds. And by we, I mean Jeff and me. Yes, Jeff worked with me the whole time, including driving this twenty-one-foot Ryder truck five hours to Jersey. Add another four-plus hours to Virginia loading and unloading, that meant 10 hour days on the road, alternating with 10 hour days trying to sell out of the warehouse.

I was the one that was always bitching how it was bullshit that it was just us who drove the truck—which could only go sixty miles an hour, was uncomfortable as hell, and most of the time the AC did not work—and we were the only ones who did all the loading and unloading of hundreds of cases.

(Some people never understood why I wore shorts and T-shirts, but this was sweaty work, regardless of the temperature. Meanwhile, Jeff always had jeans and flannel shirts and work boots. I was in okay shape from swimming and walking at least four to five days a week. Jeff probably had not worked out since his college days.)

So, that one day, I just exploded once the detail was done. I drove like a maniac to meet our team at the briefing place and jumped out of the truck screaming like a lunatic. "You motherfuckers drive in your comfy, air conditioned vehicles and stop for lunch or dinner. Once you arrive, you sit, have coffee, and when we do finally arrive with the truck, you ask, 'What the fuck took you so long?'" I called everyone useless motherfuckers who didn't do a goddamn thing while Jeff and I were busting our backs all day.

Joe Conn was a nice guy but he was not one of my favorites. He had the job of observer. He kept surveillance on us and on the bad guys. I added, "Joe, you cocksucker, you've never driven the goddamn truck or lifted one fucking case of cigs. So say it again and I'll rip your fucking head off."

Even though F-bombs were every other word in my language, Brihiem (aka Brian) stepped in. I'd known him most of my life, and the he was a really nice guy. (Brian was the best driver, and best at countersurveillance. I talk about this in the first book.) He got me to start cooling down.

Then, suddenly, Jeff Who said in the calmest voice possible, "Now you're angry."

There was dead silence for a couple seconds, then a burst of laughter from the dozen agents on site, including El Bobbo, Chief Rand, Brihiem and, yes, even me, this screaming lunatic.

All I could think of was that scene in the movie *The Wild Bunch* where William Holden, Ernest Borgnine, Ben Johnson, Warren Oates, and Edmund O'Brien are pissed off at each other because the bank robbery they'd pulled off was a setup. Gang members were shot. There was no gold in the bags, just metal washers. Suddenly, in this mass of anger, they just start laughing like crazy. Just like our outburst of laughter right then.

After that, every time someone lost it because of stress or exhaustion or just talking about something stupid an agent did that day, which was an almost daily occurrence, sooner or later you'd hear, "Now you're angry," and it always worked.

Thank you, Jeff.

[PART 6]
PTSD

[16]

LETTING THINGS GO/I TRY BUT CANNOT

I've been told by family and friends and my publicist, who have my best interest at heart, to stop watching the news and let things go, which I realize is a major factor for my anger and not good for my PTSD.

Maybe it's how I grew up, believing in right and wrong. Well, most of the time. Because my dad served in WWII and Korea and most everyone else in my family, including my brother and cousins, fought in wars, I grew up respecting and loving this country.

My dad taught me to be responsible for myself. Pay your bills, and never embarrass your family. Yes, this was the same dad who was abusive, never showing any affection.

Then throw in all those movies while growing up in the 1950s, '60s, and '70s where the good guy won and loved his country.

What was it they said? God, family, country. I believed in that and still do.

I know for a fact that my brother served with distinction. My cousin Frank put his ass on the line, too. Not just in Vietnam but for twenty-six years in numerous countries. Also, another cousin suffered injuries when his ship was bombed in combat. These guys help me with my PTSD to this day.

Then there's my Cousin Joe. As a family, we laugh about the fact that Joe is still waiting for his Purple Heart. He goes around calling himself a doctor.

Joe got his nickname from a time when another cousin, Leroy, was sick in the hospital. Joe grabbed a lab coat and clipboard and asked a nurse to see Leroy's chart. That wasn't the only time. He's done this more than once.

The first time I rode in the back of a police car I was eight and I was with "The Doctor," who was 10. We were hitchhiking on a highway trying to get to a racetrack 25 miles away to bet my haircut money, two dollars.

AFTER 9/11, MY NEVER LETTING THINGS GO BECAME EVEN more good and bad, both. The good part made me successful and a survivor; the bad contributed to my PTSD. But my psychiatrist told me to speak my mind and not keep shit inside me.

So here goes.

What the fuck happened to this country?

I am one pissed-off guy. I'm guessing every vet, first responder, nurse, social worker, and everybody else who puts themselves in danger to make this country safe feels the same way at some time or other.

What is with this belief that people with extensive criminal records should not be incarcerated? Let me know how that would work when some criminal is in your house threatening to kill your family. With the changing ways and how criminals are being released, that can happen.

This ignorant bullshit that they say about defunding the police really offends and hurts police officers, many of whom already suffer from PTSD, and keeps them from putting it all on the line to protect everyone.

I've had two speaking engagements canceled due to improper language. Improper language, really? I'd love to see those righteous bastards say, "Remember when that guy was involved in that volatile, guns-drawn situation? His last words were, 'Sir, would you mind putting the shotgun down?'"

Maybe people who complain all the time about what a bad country the USA is should think about what they can do to improve it. 'Cause life is hard, and we have to stand up for our rights.

Maybe they should bring coffee to any support group and see what these vets and first responders are like now. Because they did their best and were immensely affected in trying to make this country safer.

I could go on. Actually I did. I had a few other choice words to say about politics, but my editor cut them. She wouldn't let me say everything I really wanted to say, but just imagine I inserted a great big rant here about politics, righteous idiots, and extremists.

Okay, time for a happy pill.

Before the happy pill kicks in, I'll talk about the good politicians. Sad to say, it's mostly the grassroots ones who are in touch with their constituents because they know them; they are friends and neighbors who listen to what people have to say. Local politicians engage more and take the time to reason with people. But, most importantly, they work with other parties. Imagine that, working across the aisle for the betterment of their community. What a novel idea!

Because I travel a lot and work with so many different communities, I find this local thing to be true more times than not, especially since 9/11. I can speak more in depth with my hometown community of Utica, New York. I can be a little prejudiced because I know most of the men and even grew up with some of them, but I want to share some of the good I see in politics.

Our mayor, Robert Palmieri, is a long-time acquaintance. He's another product of East Utica, personable and, yes, tough. He claims he beat me up in high school. Yes, we actually had a fight in our library in high school. That was broken up very quickly. Besides, I can take him—at least, I know Billy the Liquor Guy can. Robbie is still a tough SOB and does not take any shit from anybody. He expects city employees to work hard. He's also a hard worker and not afraid to get his hands dirty with manual labor. Robbie also had a vision for the city, which he made come true. And yes, he works with the other party. Well, most of the time.

Next would be our county executive, Anthony Picente, who is a product of the Boulevard of Broken Dreams. If I remember right, the first time I heard that phrase was from him, many years ago. Oneida County has improved immensely since he has been in leadership.

Before you say I am sucking up, neither would hire me

when I returned to the area after my twelve-year undercover odyssey because I was not qualified for any open position.

Imagine if the state or federal government adhered to that policy instead of hiring the unqualified. That is why government, especially our federal government, is so dysfunctional.

Apparently, my happy pill hasn't totally kicked because my anger toward that shitshow is still coming through.

While I wait for the anger to disappear, I will mention a couple other politicians who have improved Utica and Oneida County. Currently, my area is fortunate to have great politicians, from both parties, who work together—yes, Republicans and Democrats working together—which is the main reason Oneida County is experiencing immense growth.

There's Assemblywoman Marianne Buttenschon. She made tough decisions to create a state budget that the state could grow with. You see her everywhere, always with a smile and positive thoughts. Believe me, she is one tough lady. One reason is because she grew up in the political arena. She's smart with common sense and another product of a tough Utica upbringing. I have seen her in confrontational situations debating intelligently, standing her ground.

Legislator Tony Leone calls himself a moderate democrat, which he is. I do enjoy breaking his balls about his political party, especially given the state and federal idiots in office. He prides himself on trying to get along with everybody. But he will always be one up on me. The first time I met Tony and I told him I worked for the state, he replied, "No, you're employed by the state." Back in the day, once he found out I worked out of town, Tony stepped up to make sure my son became included in local sports. Just because his son was friends with my son.

Tony worked in his family business his whole life. Like the politicians I mentioned prior, he knows what it is like to do an honest day's work and how to deal with the public, good and bad. I do remind Tony, quite often, at least his children became smarter, because his two sons now work for the state in law enforcement. His daughter takes after his wife because she is the smartest one, choosing to work in the private sector.

These Baby Boomers are from a generation where people actually did work together. Also, Baby Boomers understand responsibility and have a good work ethic, which was taught to us by our parents, the Greatest Generation.

Yes, Baby Boomers contributed to generations that followed us, because we tried to make it easier for our children. The problem is we made it too easy.

Yes, I babble!

Here I started on another rant about politics, but my editor cut it. Talk about being censored!

Bitching about politics is just another way I cope with PTSD. It's not as good as swimming, but it does help a lot by venting against what I feel are lies against this great country of ours. Also, I realize that the good people of America far outweigh the people that are trying to tear this country apart for whatever their agenda is. Knowing this helps a lot with my PTSD.

Learning to live with PTSD, through therapy and sessions with doctors and support groups, I have learned to express my thoughts but try to keep them under control. Especially when they escalate into rages of anger.

Also, I've learned to talk about things that make me feel good. Thus, the reason for expressing my political views, good and bad.

Through many support group sessions, I've witnessed the anger from police officers who put their lives on the line, saw friends killed in the line of duty, and so many others who suffer from PTSD for various reasons.

Now I feel better because my psychiatrist, Dr. Rayancha, was right about expressing my thoughts. (There I go name dropping again!) Thank you, Doc, for helping me to appreciate life again. I will always remember your initial advice: We live, then we die. You can be miserable or happy. Your choice.

[17]
FIRST PANIC ATTACK

At work one day, I started experiencing some conditions that definitely were not normal. I would break out in cold sweats, heart palpitations, and shortness of breath. Being stupid, thinking I was tough, I tried to deal with it. I thought it could be indigestion, along with bad gas pain, which was possible due to the fact I'd been driving all day and just had greasy drive-through food. Plus, I was rushing somewhere at over eighty miles per hour. It was kind of a normal day.

This attack was so painful, however, that I had to pull over on the shoulder, tires screeching, stones flying. I slammed my unmarked vehicle in park, jumped out of the car, and started walking back and forth on the side of the New York State Thruway. The pain felt a bit better, but it still hurt like a bastard.

Suddenly, I remembered there was some Gas-X in the

glove compartment. Kind of a cop thing, when you're sitting driving a lot. Throw into that always eating crappy drive-through food. Immediately, I swallowed three pills. Eventually, the pain started to lessen. But to be on the safe side, I took a couple of aspirin, just in case it was a heart attack—I mean the beginning of one. Yeah, now I was being smart. Yeah, right. Fucking moron, don't go to a hospital. No, just get back in the car and ignore what just happened 'cause you're Billy the Liquor Guy, Indestructible Moron.

The next week I was driving home when I had another attack. This one included hands shaking and pain in my back. Again, I was more tough than stupid. What did I do? No, I didn't call for help on the police radio, a foot from me, or drive to a hospital. Being the genius I was, I thought if I was dying, I should drive home, which was only about fifteen minutes away. Yeah, drive home, die in my driveway in front of my family! Bigger moron.

As I was pulling onto my street, the pain subsided. I parked in my driveway and got out of the car like nothing happened.

Fortunately, the third attack occurred while I was working with a partner. All of a sudden, the cold sweats started along with the intense pain in my chest. My partner was driving, and I heard, "Senior, you okay?" He never said another word, just put the red lights on and drove to the nearest hospital.

Well, when you pull up to a hospital emergency room in a cop car with red lights and a siren blaring, and add to that a guy running out with his badge around his neck and shoulder holster in plain view, screaming, "My partner needs help!" it brings a shitload of medical staff out to you. What I never heard while dealing with the intense pain was that my partner radioed ahead, saying he had an injured police officer.

Next thing I realized, I was on a gurney being wheeled into the hospital, and the medical staff was yelling, "Where were you shot?" I tried to mumble that I had not been shot. Most likely it was inaudible because they started ripping/cutting off my clothes, looking for an entry or exit wound. Of course, my partner had gone off to park the car, so he was not around to clarify things.

With the intense pain I was in, I was thinking, actually hoping, I had been shot. Because if I lived, this would be one embarrassing situation where my fellow officers would break my balls. For the rest of my career, they'd be saying things like, "Senior, show us your wound!" "Senior, show us your medal for being shot while on duty!" "Senior, how's the pain today from your bullet wound?"

You get the idea.

The only thought that brought levity is I remembered my mother saying, "Make sure you have clean underwear on. You never know when you could end up in a hospital." That advice came in my youth when I went to the hospital with a coat hanger through my left nut, due to the fact my brother and I were playing Zorro.

Back to this emergency room visit.

My partner entered the ER, and a doctor said, "Your partner has not been shot."

Dave, in his Staten Island gravelly voice, replied, "Who the *fuck* said he was shot?" That's my partner making new friends as he continued to shake his head, mumbling, "Morons." Of course, Dave ended the conversation with, "Where's my partner's firearm?"

The response from a smartass ER nurse made me smile a second time. "What fucking gun?"

Dave actually smiled and responded, "I need to secure his weapon."

The nurse told Dave, "Hold your water, Super Cop, we think your partner had a panic attack per his heart rate and BP we've run so far. We're going to run a few more tests, then we will release him if they are okay."

And after a few more tests, my diagnosis was a panic attack.

A fucking panic attack. Here we go!

I must be a fucking soothsayer, because just as I predicted, as soon as I arrived at work, the ball breaking started. Also, I was right on with the lines I had thrown at me. To add to the anger that day and my stupidity, I kept telling myself, "Billy the Liquor Guy does not have panic attacks."

What a fucking ego, and, yes, stupid. I went back to work like nothing happened. If you've read *Under Too Long*, you know I never said a word to my family about this. You might have heard/read before about me not telling my family initially about my undercover work or the incident when the gun was put to the back of my head and clicked, misfiring, either.

Within a week of returning to work, I started seeing people on the road that were not there. Of course, I never told anybody. And what did Billy the Idiot do? I just stopped driving, which was easy because I was a senior investigator. I just pulled rank and assigned that task to anyone I worked with.

Actually, my reasoning for these visions was somewhat logical. I told myself this was a delayed reaction to the vehicle accident my captain and I were in that resulted in a fatality. With this thought in my mind, I kept hearing George's last few words to me before he passed from cancer. He said, "God is punishing me for that person I killed."

My response was, "George, you know that's just not true. I know it, you know it, but more importantly, the vehicle accident investigated by New York State Police stated it was not. It was the blinding snowstorm and the individual standing in the middle of the highway, trying to help that idiot who lost control with that dog he had on his lap and ended up in the ditch. Besides, George, if God punishes people for any misdeeds they've done in their lifetime, it would not be somebody like you, Studley Do Right."—that was my nickname for George—"it would be more for people like me, Dudley Do Wrong." I've broken a lot of rules and probably a few laws before, during, and probably after my career, too. I mean, who has unsupervisable on their evaluation? Thus the name Dudley Do Wrong!

Well, the genius I am, now I started thinking, *This is God punishing me for not seeing that person standing on the highway in a blinding snowstorm on Dec. 13th at 5:36 p.m. over twenty years ago. Plus, more than a few wrong turns I took in my life.* George used to call them falters.

Thinking about you, George. I'll have another cold one. Good chance I could use one where I could end up, or maybe not.

Anyway, back to the panic attacks. For whatever reason, I started praying to God, asking/begging to help me with what I was going through. All of which would continue for ten years of pain, anger, depression, and thoughts of suicide.

I thank God, every day, for helping me deal with PTSD.

[18]

WHAT HAPPENED TO MY LIFE?

Before I continue, I have to say, from my notes on napkins, sticky notes, Marriott message pads, real-size legal pads, and rough drafts, I am having trouble remembering the chronological order of some of the events through my living hell of PTSD. I am relying on my memory, since I did not keep a journal at the beginning of this journey. So try to not get confused, like I do, if they are out of order. I do remember what happened, I'm just not sure when they actually occurred.

Okay, back to the events to the best of my knowledge—wow, that is a saying I used all during my career, either to superiors or to Internal Affairs. "I do not recollect that event at this time." Thank you, Paul Rossi, my deputy director, for the phrase, "I Have no knowledge of that incident at this time." Now back to the PTSD.

Within two months of retirement, I started experiencing these so-called panic attacks. Still denying they were panic attacks, I went to the emergency room three times and ended up with the same diagnosis each time: a panic attack.

After my fourth attack, waking up from a deep sleep in intense pain and soaked in sweat, I called my long-time physician, Dr. Ulahannan, the nicest person you could ever meet. I told him I wanted multiple medical tests and I didn't care if I had to stay in the hospital for a few days. This was about mid-June. Dr. Ulahannan said, "Well, I can get you in mid-August."

My response was, "I will kill myself by then." Yes, you're right, that's probably something you shouldn't say to a physician, even my long-time physician and a great person.

What happened next you could have predicted. Me, not so much.

An ambulance came within a few minutes, along with a state trooper car. The trooper knew I had retired from police work, so he asked, "Do you have any weapons in the house?" I did, but I could not remember exactly where. Yes, another part of my condition was my loss of memory from time to time.

So off to the hospital we went! Well, to my surprise, I went right through the admitting process, straight to a private room. I was thinking *All right, this is good.* That was until I realized they were putting restraints on my wrists. Even though I was thinking, *What the FUCK?* my response, in a calm voice, was, "Is this really necessary?"

"Sir, it's for your safety and ours," they told me, a line I'd said hundreds of times while putting handcuffs on suspects.

Even this dumb bastard knew, from the smart ones I arrested, to just keep your mouth shut and be calm.

Thank God, after numerous questions and the appearance

of my doctor, the restraints were removed. Which is funny because, since I started dealing with my PTSD over the last five years, whenever someone told me I was crazy, my response was, "Certifiable!" embellishing a bit from my diagnosis from my psychiatrist.

The rest of my stay involved multiple medical tests, daily, for the next five days: MRIs, X-rays, daily blood work and, yes, a whole shitload of poking and prodding my body. Scopes in every opening from ears to mouth to that other opening. And a hell of a lot more tests I cannot remember.

Well, I got what I asked for: a week, or just about it, in the hospital. What I didn't realize is if you go to the hospital for comfort and diagnosis, *don't*!

Other than my illness, it was the most miserable experience, ever! I was woken up all through the night when I was finally in a restful sleep. There was constant noise and the persistent smell of cleaning fluids, which I eventually was diagnosed with having a severe allergy to.

On my last day, which I did not realize it was at the time, they told me there was no medical condition that they could detect, other than maybe something viral, which I've learned is what they say when they do not find any of the regular shit.

The doctors realized I was not happy. They excused themselves, closed the curtain around my bed, asked to speak to my wife, stepped a few feet away, and started talking to her. When I heard them tell her it had to be mental, well, tossing out my filter, I yelled out, "I can hear you, you stupid bastards!"

Needless to say, my exit from the hospital was faster than my arrival.

[19]
COME AND GET MY WEAPON

Two months after my very unpleasant hospital stay, in which my exit was just as quick as my arrival because Anger Boy had made an appearance—one of a few nicknames I earned during this illness, in addition to Cuckoo, Crazy Man, and Weird Willie, Folly Boy, and a few more I wish I could forget—I knew I was really messed up. I did not care about anything—not even my family. When I did get off the couch, I shuffled when I walked. Panic attacks and fears of everything were constant. Doors shutting would make me jump. So would the doorbell ringing. Those TV tests with that blare. I would actually jump or more likely fall off the couch. I even had panic attacks when a fly came into the house. The buzzing of its wings sounded like a helicopter.

But the worst was the constant ringing of the phone. Yes, we still had landlines. The phone ringing was the reason I earned one of those nicknames, Crazy Man. Actually, it was,

"Are you fucking crazy?" the time I finally ripped the phone out of the wall.

Okay, cuckoo.

The days got worse, and thoughts of suicide floated through my mind, even with me telling myself this would never happen and I would never do that to my family. But, to be on the safe side, I called my partner and asked him to please come and get my personal weapon. Dave never asked why or when. All he said was, "Okay, I am on my way!"

Even though it was over an hour ride, Dave arrived in forty-five minutes. He probably drove his usual eighty miles an hour. I can still hear Dave, in that Staten Island tone, on the police radio, "Company Car," which is the call sign to any other police vehicle that would observe you driving an excessive speed.

By the way, I found my personal weapon in my underwear drawer. See what I mean about losing my train of thought? Obviously, you can see that issue still exists. Now, the bullets are another story. I never found those. Best guess, they got thrown out one time after Angry Boy appeared.

All David did was look at me and say, "Just let me know if you ever need anything. Call me." He knew I was not up for conversation, so he just left.

The ironic thing was I only saw him one more time, years later, to get my weapon back. Even worse, it was only for a few minutes, seeing as he was suffering from his own serious medical issues. All I said was, "Call me anytime." He never did. Sad, seeing that we'd had each other's backs for years. There were lots of laughs and good times and memories. But at the time, I couldn't give a shit.

One last thought: I just remembered that, of the ten original guys on the undercover ops, four had to surrender their weapons due to psychiatric care. Nick at Night, and of course The Deer Slayer. Actually, it was his duty weapon. I guess someone had heard from him. I was the third. The fourth, I cannot remember who it was.

There goes that memory thing again!

[20]
FLASHBACKS!

Okay, to calm down Crazy Man, and before I get to issues that will definitely bring Angry Boy out, it's time for my happy pills and a Jack Daniel's and Coke…

Now I've had my Jack Daniel's, which has helped, and I'm just waiting on my happy pills to help deal with my anger when it kicks in.

The incident with the gun held to my head comes out occasionally. I definitely try to keep that tucked away in the back of my brain. But when you're a cop who has had a gun pointed at your head, it frequently comes out in memories, and is pretty vivid. But it does not last long.

The one movie I will never watch again is *The Departed*, where the undercover officer is played by Leonardo DiCaprio. Even though I'm not a big fan, he did a great job playing a conflicted undercover agent. Like me, DiCaptrio's Billy Costigan character was raised in a mob environment, so he was able to infiltrate Frank "Whitey" (Buller) Costello's inner circle. The reason I will never watch again is because the undercover agent and most of his team were killed. Yes, it's a movie, but to me, it was too close to the life I led, so it did cause a flashback that was too close to reality.

Okay, my happy pill is kicking in, which will make the next flashback easier to deal with. Even though the pill makes me feel weak and stupid and, yes, crazy.

One of the worst of flashbacks comes when my grandkids, great nephews, and great nieces play with fake guns or anything that resembles a gun. The ones that shoot foam bullets are the worst. The first time they pointed a fake gun, pulled the trigger, and it did not fire, I really lost it. Crazy Man and Angry Boy all in one. Kids are always going around with fake guns, and to repeat the Christmas episode, one of the fake guns went off by my head. I caught myself before I went into full rage mode, and got up and went for a walk. Most of the time, my son or daughter have the guns put away when I return.

Another flashback that appeared constantly for years is the accident in that blinding snowstorm on December 13th, 1998, at 5:36 p.m., now over twenty years ago. The first snowstorm of every winter, it definitely hits me, even more so if I drive by the scene of the accident, no matter what the weather is like. It took me years to finally drive again at night when it's snowing.

Actually, my fear of riding in a snowstorm has occurred multiple times. The first was in college, riding with my friend Mario to Buffalo in my brother's 340 Duster. After the bars closed in Utica, Mario lost control of the car in a snowstorm. The cause, which we found out later that two dumb college kids had no idea about, was a Duster had no weight in the ass end, which made it shitty in the winter with that 340 engine.

The second time was my first day on the job with PATB. My training officer and future partner Dave was, of course, speeding down the thruway well above the speed limit, especially considering the snowy conditions. But what can I say to a senior investigator on the first day on the job? We were heading westbound when Dave spotted a trooper going east. Again, Dave, in that gravely tone he had, relayed on the radio, “Company Car.” The trooper responded, “Don’t expect me to respond when you wipe out!” Not two minutes later, we were doing 360s down the thruway.

Yes, I’m rambling. The happy pill has kicked in, and per my psychiatrist’s instructions, I’m expressing my fears.

The third snowstorm terror I was being transported to Binghamton from Syracuse by a trooper, just days after he completed his probationary period. I believed the trooper was approaching a curve too fast, so I said, “Troop, think you should slow down a bit?”

He responded, “I got this, Senior.” He was just finishing his sentence and there we went. Our car did 360s southbound on NYS I-81. The trooper was so embarrassed I did not even read him the riot act.

I went on about these accidents because of all the danger I’d been through. I still get panic attacks while riding or driving in snowstorms.

So much for an undercover agent with no fear.

Highways have not been kind to me either.

In 2001, the summer before 9/11, I was driving back to the Plattsburgh office on a lazy Sunday afternoon after a swim in Schroon Lake. About ten miles north of Schroon Lake on Rte. 87, I saw multiple cars pulled over on both sides of the road. Once I stopped, I saw at least six people screaming and running around the median. What I observed, once exiting my vehicle, was horrific. I won't go through the details again, seeing I discussed it earlier in this book, but the scenes of brains splattered on highways and bodies lying all over the median, with multiple serious injuries, including one male almost cut in half on the southbound guard rail, have stuck with me.

Even before 9/11, I'd seen enough death and mutilated bodies for ten lifetimes and had a damn good reason to suffer from flashbacks.

Even though these are horrible memories, the one scene, in my mind, that I know will last till the day I die does not even involve a dead body. It was the scene of the jagged facing structure of the World Trade Center, which most people have seen in photos. I saw it, unfortunately, from a few hundred feet away. Even worse was knowing that thirty-nine of my coworkers were buried underneath that rubble that most people refer to as The Pile.

These flashbacks have haunted me for dozens of years, and counting. But due to a positive attitude, therapy groups, and exercise, I deal with them. My happy pills and just a bit of Jack Daniel's daily helps, too.

[21]
GROUNDHOG DAY/MY LIVING HELL

Like I said, PTSD was a living hell. Mainly because it was like Groundhog Day.

Initially, it wasn't because of my earlier doctor's determinations, which included mono, then Meniere's Disease, a viral infection, bitten by a tick, or a bad case of the flu. One of the best was an Agent Orange diagnosis. When I told this quack, "But I wasn't in Vietnam," his response was, and I quote, "Are you sure?"

By this time, I'd definitely lost faith in doctors. So I turned to holistic medicine, eating just beans, greens, and grains, seaweed, tofu; meditation; and coffee enemas. These were all good for losing close to a hundred pounds, which I could not even enjoy because it didn't help with the PTSD (though people said I looked great). Even my buddy Syro said, "Don't know what you have, but kiss me so I can get it!"

I was in constant pain and felt like I was dying. What was that saying? First I was afraid I was dying, then after a while I was afraid I was not. That's how I felt. After all the medical tests, for the next year and then some, every day was the same. Nightmares all night of horrific visions, from being eaten alive to thousands of bees stinging me to being hung over and over to falling off a skyscraper in NYC. That last one I could figure out. Along with the one about being shot in the head.

I do have thoughts about being hung, but I'll keep that one to myself. Hint: past crimes in a previous life. Some people would say I was crazy. Imagine that!

Whatever time I might have fallen asleep, I cannot tell you how many nights I woke up and the clock said 5:55 a.m. Of course, I was in cold sweats. Then, when I finally had enough strength to get out of bed, within minutes, I had nausea, body aches, and intense pain throughout my body, pain that felt like a thousand knives stabbing me! I eventually read somewhere about hot baths with salt, then sea salt, and working up to rock salt. Sounded crazy to me, but I tried it and it did help a bit.

Then there was the issue that my body felt like it was burning up. To remedy this, first, I would sit on the front porch in mid-winter with just a T-shirt and windbreaker, shorts, and sneakers. Eventually I started to walk around my block in the same outfit with my dog, Willie, mostly between two a.m. and six a.m. Poor Willie, about the third time I took him for a walk late at night or in the early morning hours, he had to be looking at me and thinking, "You crazy bastard! Are you kidding me?"

Months later, a neighbor, who did not sleep much either, told me he would see me out walking with shorts and a T-shirt. Yes, he did tell me I was crazy!

Actually, scalding hot baths and winter walks, in whiteouts, did help. But the reprieve never lasted. So Groundhog Day continued until, after two years, I finally did seek psychiatric help. I wish I would have done it sooner, mainly because what I learned about putting other thoughts in my brain, which helps me not to focus on all the negative shit. Of course, the medications did help a lot too. But it took months to find the right mixture to start working.

I learned to say and believe stuff like function till five once I got up, meaning I only had to make it through what would be a regular workday and not a full 24 hours. It made the day seem shorter; it lessened the late nights. I used my winter walks and scaring the neighbors. And since those are not possible, even in Upstate New York, for at least eight months, I took to taking ice-cold showers while singing verses of "Amazing Grace," "Red River Valley," and numerous songs from movies. This definitely kept my mind occupied, concentrating on the song while freezing myself.

And when these did not work as well as I hoped, I would yell out to the man upstairs, "Yes, I am still here, you *bastard*!" Yes, another movie reference. Steve McQueen, in *Papillion*.

Eventually, things improved where I could see that light at the end of the tunnel. It did take another couple years to live, laugh, and love life again. Thanks to my therapist, support groups, family and friends, and yes, good drugs, I am finally able to appreciate living again.

[22]

SUICIDE ATTEMPT

I've been putting off writing this chapter for so many reasons. Embarrassment for my family, knowing that I gave up—which is something I never EVER did before! It hurts even more that this was the most important decision in my life, and I failed my family and, most importantly, *myself!*

How I ever could have considered suicide is something, at this time, I cannot comprehend.

Sure, I could use the excuse of the constant mental anguish and physical pain. Yes, it was a living hell every day for years. The same with depression and fear. Then throw in the anger of *why me?* I saw everyone around me enjoying themselves, laughing, engaged in conversation, while I was in constant fear, ostracizing myself, physically and mentally, from everybody.

Well, I could have said bullshit to all these excuses, but the fact was I could not. That would be lying to myself and all the other PTSD sufferers. This disease does bring the strongest of us all to our knees, crying, begging, and praying for some relief. The only way you deal with this illness is to reach into yourself for strength. Pray, get help from professionals, take one day at a time or even part of a day at a time, and find something positive in each day! If not, suicide can become a reality.

Suicide is a permanent solution to a temporary problem. Yes, PTSD can be temporary, at least the constant horror. If you really work at it, with all the ways I have mentioned, you will be able to live—the key word is "live"—with PTSD every day of your life. PTSD has one of the highest suicide rates. That's a fact. If you are experiencing PTSD, please address it and learn how to live with it. Believe me, *you can*!

I *did*, and I am a bit of a whiny ass. The first time I dialed the New York State Healthcare Line for Mental Health, my eyes were full of tears.

Yes, this badass, Billy the Liquor Guy, who saw his share of danger throughout his undercover career, not only considered suicide, but attempted it!

This is the first time I was able to *write these words*. Which is ironic because, while talking to other PTSD sufferers, I started my talks with first responders, who I knew were ordered to be at my presentation, and were probably thinking, *Okay, you have to sit here and listen to cop stories from this burned-out old cop, believing what he thinks are his days of fame.*

I opened with, "Who has had some recent bad days on the job?" At least half the room raised their hands. Next, I asked, "Who has been feeling the stress and pressures of the job for the last year or so?" Now only one or two raised their hands.

Then I asked, "Who has had suicidal thoughts?" I raised my hand. Then I added, "I not only thought about it, I *attempted* it! My job was no more tough than your job, and I am a tough bastard who is from the old school of policing." I'd just told them I knew how tough this job was. That definitely got their attention.

Eventually, they did ask me what work I did. I told them I worked on an undercover detail after 9/11. More than a few in the room realized who I was. This gave me more credibility, but more importantly, it brought that cop humor into play. Like, "*Wow*, that picture of you must be taken at least thirty years ago," or "Your undercover work started about twenty years ago. You were a bit old to do that shit!"

Once they stopped breaking my balls, I told them that sick cop humor could help them get through the day, especially in dealing with death. But it also contributed to my PTSD, because utilizing that as a coping mechanism suppressed all my thoughts and fears that exploded when I retired.

I told them what my psychiatrist, Dr. Rayancha, said, that your brain is like a rubber band, it can only deal with so much strain before it breaks. Then I added what he stated to me after every session: "We all live and die. You can live your life happy and enjoy it, or live miserable and die."

The one thing that happened after every group session was at least one person hung around. Most of the time, it was two or three. We'd sit down, have a cup of coffee. If it was one, I'd wait for him to ask, "So how long did you have these suicidal thoughts?" If it was a couple of people, I'd initiate the conversation with the question, "Would any of you be interested in knowing how long I had these thoughts of suicide before trying to act on it?" This smaller group always responded by nodding their heads in a positive reply.

I explained how I'd tried everything I heard or read about depression, first telling them how I called my partner to come and get my weapon. Even at the early stages, I knew something was wrong with all the flashbacks. I'd talk about my crazy-ass winter walks, the bizarre herbs and rituals I tried, including eating scrapings of deer antlers or injecting special herbs, both of which were disgusting. But I tried them because somebody somewhere said they helped.

I even tried thousand-year-old Chinese remedies and Dr. Sherry Rogers' allergy procedures, which involved the most extensive bloodwork I'd ever gone through—hundreds of needle pricks in a two-day period. It was very painful, but it did detect that I was totally depleted of numerous minerals my body was supposed to have. Of course, all the MDs I saw said this was not accepted by medical science.

One thing I do know is my blood pressure, sugar levels, and cholesterol readings all *improved*! Even though I realized this most likely occurred through my diet, since nutritionists had gotten me to only eat tofu, kale, beans, greens, and grains.

Mentally, though, there was no improvement. The reason I explained this to the men I was talking to was to show that PTSD sufferers will try anything that could possibly help.

Also, it's a start. The Chinese believe you improve your body and mind from your inside, and balance will improve your health. If I could go as far as doing coffee enemas, I don't want to hear any bullshit excuses. I say, start today dealing with your PTSD and work on enjoying life *again*!

When asked the question by the group, "What made you

finally decide to attempt to commit suicide and how were you going to do it and what happened that you did not go through with it?" I first said, like most suicides, I was just tired of living like that. I felt it was not living, and I didn't want to be a burden. So one day I just said, "FUCK IT." I got up off the couch, shuffled down the hallway... and as I passed our entranceway, I heard knocking on the tiny windows around the front door. My cousin Frank, who I had not seen in three decades, was there.

Obviously, I answered the door, dazed and confused, and I guess relieved. Frank heard I was really sick, so he just stopped in. I decided right there, between the asshole putting a gun to my head that misfired and this almost attempt, those were two signs I was not meant to die yet. I wasn't going to wait for a third. So I told myself what my team said to anybody who said they couldn't take the job anymore: "Go to your safe, open it, take your balls out, and put them back on!"

I won't lie, the next two years were tough! At least five days a week, Cousin Frank would come and pick me up and drag my ass out and make sure we went somewhere, whether it was to a doctor appointment, to visit somebody, or just for a ride, anywhere. We met once a week with cousins and two friends.

So thanks, Cousin Frank, Cousin Joe "The Doctor," Cousin Leroy, and Cousin Bill. And the two grandfathered in, Jeff Who and Timmy, the craziest trooper I ever met, who responded to a suspicious package call and shook it to see if it was a bomb. Which it was, and it detonated later!

Thank you guys for helping in my recovery!

I still have Billy the Liquor Guy!

[23]

LONG ROAD BACK

Once I finally realized I had PTSD, I went into my survivor mode, which I had done all through my life: in childhood, to deal with physical and mental abuse; in my adolescent years, playing sports in high school; and in college, having constant fear over how my mother was doing; then during my undercover years, to stay alive. So I just said, "I can do this too, with persistence and patience."

First was counseling and support groups. It took me months to find a therapist I was comfortable with. Thinking about it now, I'm just realizing my therapist resembled Tom Stanton. Even his mannerisms were the same. I'll let the experts figure out if this is just another reason I'm cuckoo.

Come on, you have to laugh. But I still have all the guided meditation CDs that he made for me. I have to tell you, at the beginning, not much helped. Eventually, I knew I was improving because I could be in Crazy Boy mode, but by the time I finished listening to a CD, I was relaxed. The one that works the best for me is *Walking Through the Woods*. It is 20 minutes long, and guides you to imagine seeing, hearing, and even smelling nature.

I still remember one time I did get pissed off at my therapist. Actually, on the first visit, which was almost my last, the therapist asked, "So what are you afraid of?"

My response was "Everything."

He replied, "What is your biggest fear?"

I said, "Being out in public and having a panic attack and passing out."

His response: "So someone will help you."

I said, "Obviously, we live in two different worlds."

The only reason I did go back was to pick up more relaxation CDs. But I did cancel the next two appointments. By the third one, I realized his recorded voice did relax me, so I started sessions again.

I did tell him that he was wrong about someone helping you if you fell or curled up on the ground or passed out. Thank God Billy the Liquor Guy was still in me! So we agreed to disagree. Not really, but he never pushed it, and I never mentioned it again.

In *Under Too Long*, I did discuss support groups, so I'll just give a short synopsis. It took me weeks to agree to attend a support group, which was advised by both my psychiatrist and my treating therapist. It was amazing that I eventually went, because this was the most scared I'd ever been, including any time during my undercover work. I was literally shaking when I walked into the basement of that church. Thank God a gentleman wearing an army jacket came up to me, because I was ready to bolt.

"Where did you serve?" he asked.

Bam, the biggest question I'd feared being asked in the first minute. Because I did not serve in the military, I felt I did not belong at this support group. Thank God I still had some of that Billy the Liquor Guy inside me. I just said, "My therapist said first responders were welcome. But if I am not, I'll leave." And I turned around to go.

Before I took one step, this vet, who looked like he had been to hell and back too, said, "We're all brothers in arms here. Grab a coffee and sit down anywhere."

Within seconds of sitting down, another vet, this one wearing a Vietnam hat, said, "So, new guy, is this your first meeting?" I figured the lost look in my eyes, plus my hands shaking while I was trying to drink my coffee, gave it away.

"Yes, it is," I responded.

"So tell us your name and a little bit about yourself."

"My name is Bill. I worked thirty-seven years in law enforcement, the last ten working undercover after the planes flew into the Towers, where my home office was."

"Holy shit, dude!" were the first words I heard. Then, "What agency did you work for?"

I said, "Name it and I worked for it!"

More questions were thrown at me from most of the group. If you read my first book, there's no need for me to repeat all that. The only important thing I said was, "Gentlemen, I'm guessing we all saw our share of shit. But after I retired, I went into a deep hole for years and now I'm trying to crawl out of it. Thought I'd start here. So far, it seems like a good start."

As I continued to go to these meetings, I was able to talk about the anger and depression. And, yes, the suicide shit.

To all my brothers and sisters in law enforcement, please address the possibility you have PTSD. Because if you think you can deal with it alone, YOU CAN'T!

Or if you think, *I'm a tough SOB, and that shit on the job won't affect me,* IT WILL! And believe me, we're all not as strong as we think we are.

Please don't be ashamed. SEEK HELP! Because after living with PTSD for all these years, I'm so damn tired of hearing of cops eating their guns. If anybody out there is starting to have these fears, reach out to a close friend or a support group.

If you don't feel comfortable doing either of those, contact me through my email,

Willie6868uc@gmail.com.

[24]
SWIMMING AND POLAR PLUNGES

I also strongly recommend you find something you loved to do before PTSD. It doesn't matter if it's long walks, talking to yourself, or counting the stars. Just do it, every day. Better yet, multiple times a day. This will help keep your mind busy so you're not focused on anger and depression all the time. At the beginning, this reprieve might only last a few minutes, but it's a start! I promise, it will last longer and longer the more you do it!

Swimming was the one thing that got me through verbal and mental abuse through my childhood and through all the bullshit in my adult life. Especially the PTSD. Once I got my balls back enough to jump in the pool, for the first time in years, I was never so scared in my life. I was literally shaking so much the Rome, NY YMCA lifeguard, Sadie, asked me if I was okay. I just nodded my head and jumped in. I was still terrified the entire time I swam just one lap. I finished that lap and sobbed like a baby.

Swimming made me think about living again. Even writing about swimming gives me the courage to revisit my suicide attempt.

To all my brothers and sisters who suffer from this horrible affliction of PTSD, please listen with all your heart and soul and believe living your life to the best of your ability IS ALL THAT MATTERS. Sure, you might receive support from family and friends, but life goes on for everyone. Most other people's concerns will fade because they have their own lives. So it will be up to you to push through, every day, and utilize anything (ideally healthy) that gets you through the day.

Besides swimming, little things I did might have been stupid, crazy, or mean, but they did help. I would watch birds land in a tree and count how long before they flew away. I would tell myself that every day, once I woke up, I just needed to make it to 11:11 a.m. At that point, making it to five was too much, and that seemed like a magical number. Then I'd work on making it to 11:11 p.m. When I did, I felt I had accomplished something. When anger would not loosen its grip, I'd shout out, "I am still here, *you bastard*!" and tell everyone out loud, in private, to go fuck themselves. Basically, I let fatigue fight fatigue and fear fight fear, and definitely anger fight anger.

Okay, because I ramble, I'll get back to the swimming.

Swimming helped me *immensely*! During my childhood, I was the chubby kid who played right field in youth baseball. All you Baby Boomers will understand that. But in a pool, I could swim faster and longer than all my friends. This continued throughout my whole life. In the water, I was fearless, whether it was a lake or the ocean. In a lake, I would swim to a point and back and not along the shore. Yes, through boat traffic. In St. Thomas, or Curacao, even off the coast of Africa, I would swim out to cruise ships in their port, around them, and back. Yes, I had a few fin sightings. Needless to say, when I got back on the beach, more than a few comments were made. Most of the words were, "Stupid moron," or "What's wrong with that guy?" Fuck them! Let them try to do it!

Now I'm angry!

Speaking of angry, swimming works the best for me for that. When I had a bad day, I would find a lake and swim sprints for about an hour. Or in a pool, I'd swim two thousand yards in sprints, a couple of five hundred yards, then five two hundred yards. That anger would turn to fatigue and a relaxing state when I was done with that workout.

I was once so pissed off at a couple of my bosses and a couple of other suits while swimming in a police Olympics, I would scream out their names, underwater, through the whole five hundred yard race. I can only imagine what the other swimmers thought, if they heard me. Oh well, like Jeff Who and El Bobbo would say, "You got issues." Screw my issues. I WON the heat.

One positive thing about PTSD and how it affected me is my body always felt like it was on fire. So lake swimming for all twelve months of the year was not that hard. December, January, and February were just polar plunges. But besides cooling my body down, it gave me confidence and a feeling of toughness. Due to my competitive nature, of course I had to be the first one in and the last one out of the polar plunge.

Please know this: PTSD is the fight of your life. I believe you fight it with patience and persistence and, yes, smiles and brains. Most important: DON'T EVER GIVE UP! Because I guarantee you will smile again and you will enjoy every day again. Yes, there will be ups and downs, but the ups will far exceed the downs.

One last thing: I must thank the Rome YMCA Aquatics Department, which was initially responsible for getting me on the path to recovery, and continues to support me to this day! There's Nancy, my first instructor. When I shuffled around the pool deck and told her I had medical issues, some physical and some mental, and I wasn't sure how much I could do, she told me, "That's okay! You just do what you can and move at your own pace!" Thank God because her ball of energy never stopped moving to salsa music and encouraging everyone throughout my first hour-long class.

Karen was first a classmate, then an instructor. She was another Energizer Bunny who brought her classes to a higher level, and was supportive and always asked me how I was doing.

Gail put up with my ball breaking during her classes once I started to feel better.

The lifeguards, John, Alan, and Paul, kept asking me for years, "Are you okay? Are you sure?" because the chlorine gave me an allergic reaction that made my face so red they thought I was having a heart attack.

Last but not least, Sadie was the youngest lifeguard, but she was so professional. She was friendly but never deviated from the pool rules. She was definitely my favorite one, because her last name, Falcone, was the same as my grandfather's capo when he was a soldier in that career. Second, she could have saved me, anytime, because she was the best lifeguard!

[25]

9/11 TAKES ANOTHER ONE

One of my *best friends* was buried *yesterday*, November 8, 2022, and I am hurting and pissed. I have to blame something. What makes it worse is in the past month, this is the second of my coworkers from my office of five from Plattsburgh, NY, who died of cancer.

It's hard to believe it's been over twenty-five years since I was assigned to the Plattsburgh office. The first thing I noticed was this big kid. How could you miss him? He was six foot four, at least, and three hundred pounds. He was strong and had the biggest smile I'd ever seen.

Chad's passing hit me so hard that I am still trying to cope with it. I knew he was in the fight of his life with his cancer, and he fought so hard, and most of the time kept that big smile, even through all the intense pain he endured constantly.

I decided to use the lessons I've learned in how to cope with PTSD from the past almost fifteen years in writing this chapter: express your feelings, but most importantly, think about the good times.

First, there was all the crazy shit he did that made me laugh. Chadly, as I called him, always insisted on going through the door first when we were conducting an arrest. One day, I said, "Go ahead, makes sense because you are [built like] a fucking door."

He turned, looked at me, smiled, and said, "I am," with that big laugh of his. I swear to God we were still laughing going through the door, and obviously the bad guys had strange expressions on their faces. Of course, with Man Mountain Dean, another term I lovingly called Chad, there was very little resistance.

If you've read or seen the cover of *Under Too Long*, Chad is the large African American gentlemen with the eighteen-inch-plus arms. Which brings me to a story of how intimidating and funny Chadly could be. One time we raided a bar near the Canadian border, definitely a country bar. Well, the first thing that the bartender said when he saw Chad was, "You must be lost, boy." I was thinking, *Here we go*, because all the patrons were white and rednecks. I made this assumption by their dress and lack of teeth, and by the ones sitting at the bar who laughed at the bartender's comment.

My hand was on my weapon when Chadly went into his Eddie Murphy routine. (Yes, I am a movie buff!) Chad shouted out, "I hate white people," and continued to say, "all you rednecks with no teeth, put your hands on the bar. Yes, that is all you motherfuckers." Then he showed that big smile and started that loud laugh. By far, it was the funniest arrest I was ever involved in.

I'll finish my tribute to Chadly, and all the others I've lost, with the time I received a phone call, one Sunday evening, when Chad said, "Billy, I shot myself."

Seeing Chad was so calm, I responded, "On purpose?"

"No, I was at the firing range with a lady, teaching her to shoot a weapon." Chadly was also the agency's firearms instructor.

I said, "Explain, please."

"Well, you know, Billy, I was showing off to the young lady, and I put up some metal targets. One of my shots ricocheted and hit me in the chest."

Of course, I inquired, "Are you hurt?"

"Not really. The bullet just hit my flesh on my chest. But it does not hurt."

"Chad, is the bullet still in your chest?"

"Not really," he responded. "I pulled it out."

I didn't know if he was the toughest son of a bitch I'd ever heard of or if the bullet was only a ricochet and had lost most of its velocity, but my response was, "Do you have your personal car or a company car [police vehicle]?"

"Billy, you know I'm not that stupid." Meaning, he knew better than to have any civilian, especially a woman, riding in his police vehicle without authorization.

I was thinking, *That is debatable.*

"I have my personal vehicle," Chad said.

"Okay. Have your lady friend drive you to the hospital and have it checked out."

Before he hung up, he asked, "What should I say on my report?"

"Let's see what the hospital says about the injury," I said. "Then we will discuss the report."

If you are asking how I could be so calm with this, this was not the weirdest thing I'd experienced with Chadly. There's more to come in my next book, including a story about Chad being mistaken for a bear while we were chasing a smuggler on foot through a wooded area on the USA/Canadian border. Definitely in the top three of my thoughts about Chadly.

Okay, writing about the good times with Chadly helped, and I did not even need a happy pill or Jack Daniel's this time!

On the other hand, there were a couple things that did put me into a spiral, into the dark hole of PTSD, which includes flashbacks, anger, and depression.

First, the one that really pissed me off was Chad fought this horrible cancer disease with all the intense pain and mental anguish for what seemed like an eternity. But when everything he could do to fight it was done, he said, "I just want to go home and be as comfortable as possible while confronting the inevitable." Well, after only one day in hospice and pain free, thanks to the marvels of medicine, he died.

Second, and this is a regret. With Chadly I thought of him as a friend but most of that was as two cops working together. Well, in his last few months, I did get to know Chad.

At his funeral, I was fortunate to meet friends and family who thought Chad was Superman. Between all the tears, you could see smiles and hear laughter. There is no shame in saying three tough-ass agents—Jeff Who, Nick at Nite, and I—shed tears, along with our share of laughter, when they played the video of Chad's life. Also, when "Amazing Grace" was played by a bagpiper at Chad's gravesite, a lot of eyes were full of tears, especially all the law enforcement present.

Yes, I regret not knowing until the end about the full life Chad lived in the short fifty-one years he was on God's green earth! But it helped to know all he accomplished in those fifty-one years. THANK YOU, Chadly, for being my friend and showing me to enjoy each day, as it could be your last, because someday it will be.

But the thing I am most grateful for is getting to know your sister, Shawnee. She is one of the most beautiful people I've ever met. Through her, I was able to know the real Chad: musician, preacher, trainer (through his gym), but more importantly, a positive influence and mentor to so many people.

Also, bro, to have someone like Shawnee with you at your side all the time, dealing with this most difficult part of your life, was a blessing. Just to let my readers know, Shawnee, his little sister, quit her job so she could take care of her big brother. God bless you, Shawnee. Sadly, because I was going through my PTSD, I couldn't be there for Chad as much as I wanted to.

Chad, I know you and NASCAR racer Eddie Hawk are telling stories and laughing about remembering when. I will always remember the time we were driving down Rugar Street, near his apartment, when he told me he could roll out of a car going up to twenty miles an hour. I looked at him and shook my head. He said, "No! Watch!" Then he rolled out of the car and did it!

Yes, I did work with some crazy bastards!

I want to dedicate this book to Chad and so many others who, throughout my journey to hell and back, reminded me to be strong and have faith. THANK YOU, Chad, and save a seat for me at the Crazy Cop Table.

www.ingramcontent.com/pod-product-compliance
Lightning Source LLC
Chambersburg PA
CBHW062131020426
42335CB00013B/1177

* 9 7 8 1 9 5 8 7 2 7 5 4 6 *